MARRIAGE
AFTER
ADDICTION

TAKE BACK YOUR LIFE

TOGETHER

MARRIAGE AFTER ADDICTION

TAKE BACK YOUR LIFE
TOGETHER

ERIC KENNEDY

XO
PUBLISHING

ISBN: 978-1-960870-29-2 Paperback
ISBN: 978-1-960870-30-8 eBook

XO Publishing is a leading creator of relationship-based resources. We focus primarily on marriage-related content for churches, small group curriculum, and people looking for timeless truths about relationships and overall marital health. For more information on other resources from XO Publishing, visit XOPublishing.com.

XO Marriage®, an imprint of XO Publishing
1021 Grace Lane
Southlake, Texas 76092

Every effort is made to provide accurate URLs at the time of printing for external or third-party Internet websites, neither the author nor the publisher assume any responsibility for changes or errors made after publication.

Printed in the United States of America
24 25 26 27—5 4 3 2 1

DEDICATION

To my wife, Kristen: You have loved me perfectly when I have been far from perfect. I love being your husband.

And to my kids, Cameron, Christian, and Charlee Kate: You give me reasons to try harder every day. I love being your dad.

TABLE OF CONTENTS

ACKNOWLEDGMENTS

I extend my heartfelt gratitude to my family and friends for their unwavering support throughout my life. To my parents, Leon and Debbie Kennedy, and my brother, Travis Kennedy: You are my true heroes.

A special thank you to the XO Marriage team for their guidance and leadership. To Brent Evans, Jimmy Evans, John Andersen, and Jenny Morgan: Your insightful feedback and dedication shaped this manuscript into its best form. I am so appreciative of the staff and team at XO Marriage. I am so thankful to be a part of your family.

Thank you to Austin Davis with Clearfork Academy for your research and clinical input that went into the book and gives it validity.

I am so grateful for the generous support that made this book possible—those who believed in this project and provided invaluable resources and encouragement throughout the writing process. To Gary and Sue Youtsey, Troy and Nancy Akers, Dave and Ashley Willis, and Larry and Kristen Price: Thank you for going above and beyond. Your support, guidance, and influence have been instrumental in bringing this book to fruition.

Finally, I am immensely grateful to Dr. Marty and Patty Baker for being my pastors. Their belief in me and my recovery is why I am who I am today. To the staff and members of Stevens Creek Church: Thank you.

INTRODUCTION

When Addiction Interrupts a Marriage

Think back to your wedding day when you pledged "I do" before God and all the people you love. At the time, those vows embodied the unconditional love and deep conviction you had as you married your spouse. Now, blindsided by the unexpected reality of addiction, you stand at the frontlines of a battle to reclaim your sacred covenant with your spouse.

In the fairy-tale days of your new beginning, you likely didn't visualize all the future battles you would need to fight to keep the fire of passion lit. You couldn't foresee how trauma would threaten to snuff out the flame. Yet by grace here you remain—brave, broken, desperate, and determined to reclaim the marriage you promised to each other on your wedding day.

Building an incredible marriage takes effort—just ask any couple who's been together for a long time. Even without dealing with addiction, all marriages require commitment, patience, communication skills, and humility to thrive long-term.

Now throw the chaos of addiction into the mix.

Substance abuse and other compulsive behaviors don't just hijack a single individual. Addiction's fallout directly harms the spouse and even the entire family. Deceit shatters trust. Irrational mood swings leave non-addicted spouses feeling either ignored or attacked. Promises made end up broken while money mysteriously vanishes. Gradually, the addiction becomes the absolute center around which the rest of the relationship orbits. In many ways, it's like an unwanted third party has started running your lives.

Supportive, non-addicted spouses often walk on eggshells because they want to maintain some semblance of normalcy. They may be trying to prevent the next outburst or the disappearance of the addicted spouse altogether. Meanwhile, the addicted spouse grows more impatient, irrational, and detached over time as addiction's grip tightens.

Both spouses start building up walls, misinterpreting each other's words, grieving dreams that now seem impossible, and questioning whether the relationship is worth saving anymore at all.

Without major changes, most marriages torn apart by addiction eventually crumble. As a consequence, substance abuse and addiction lead to much higher divorce rates.[1] The odds feel totally stacked against you. Years of accumulated resentment and distrust won't disappear easily. Repairing extensive damage requires tremendous courage, exhausting emotional work, and mountains of patience.

Thankfully, there's hope and help available, but repairing a smashed relationship demands full commitment from both spouses. Halfway efforts go nowhere. It's a long, intense road to rebuild broken trust and intimacy. However, with dedication and the right resources, your love can survive. Don't give up yet!

This book contains tools you both will need to stay fortified as you navigate through some uncharted minefields. I offer no quick fixes or magical formulas—only an invitation to open your hands and hearts to each other once again. Even if you are blinking through tears right now, your willingness to lean in and make the effort opens the possibility for your marriage to receive a miracle.

So, as we begin this book together, breathe easy. Your story isn't over. In fact, the flame is still dancing. I know that is true because you are brave enough to take this issue head on, and that's why you're reading this book. Take courage—healing is available for you and your marriage if you are willing to receive it.

Addiction Isn't Your Final Chapter

Addiction.

Is there anything good about that word? Personally, I can't think of anything. Addiction is soul-crushing for everyone involved. For a spouse, watching your partner battle substance dependency or other addictive habits leaves you feeling helpless. But research shows addiction literally hijacks brain pathways, so try not to take their behaviors personally. Your partner isn't "choosing" drugs, alcohol, or other addictive behaviors over you or your marriage. Rather, their neural circuitry has been disrupted, making quitting extremely hard.

The good news is professional help combined with an empathetic support system creates pathways to freedom. I have written this book as a resource for your journey. If you go through it together, I believe it will help you address some of the major struggles in your marriage.

Of course, you can go through the book alone, but it will be so much better if both of you get a copy, read the chapters, answer the individual questions, and discuss the questions for couples. Though almost impossible alone, recovery is so possible together. Addiction does not get to write the final chapter of your marriage—at least not without a vicious fight. So, arm yourself! Start by educating yourself on setting boundaries to avoid enabling, which actually prolongs addiction. If you are the supporting spouse, practice speaking truth with love and encourage your spouse toward treatment options. With patience and open communication, stand by their side through relapses, celebrating every little win and each step in the right direction.

Healing is like a rollercoaster track rather than a linear process. There will be battles ahead. But where brokenness once overshadowed your relationship, light is available if you will only chase after it.

Who Am I to Give Advice?

How am I qualified to offer guidance to couples facing addiction? Fair question. Like many people, addiction ravaged my own life and relationships for many years until I finally got sober. I've walked the hard road back to health and purpose after hitting rock bottom. I don't claim to have all the answers, but I have plenty of scars.

I'm not some guru who magically overcame addiction or mastered relationships. I battle flaws and doubts just like anyone else. Consider me a companion who can point you to what helped me heal and find freedom. I fumbled through countless mistakes that I hope you can avoid on your journey. If I knew back then what I do now about setting boundaries, managing emotions, reaching out for support, and communicating openly, perhaps I could have spared myself and my loved ones so much pain.

Nevertheless, everything I learned through loads of tough experiences allows me to pass on hard-won wisdom to you. I share my story, including all the ways I failed, so you can discover hope. My goal here isn't self-promotion—I sincerely want to help you avoid unnecessary relationship struggles. Let my journey give you courage that no matter how broken things feel today, brighter days lie ahead if you persevere.

Keeping the Focus on Healing

Are healing and freedom really possible? Yes, I believe they are, but don't get lost in the weeds. In the addiction healing world, there are often useless debates about whether people can fully break free from substance dependency or other compulsive behaviors. Folks argue over labels and say, "You're always an addict; you just learn to manage it." Others say, "I'm a former addict. I've been completely healed." But I'm not here for unhelpful word games.

Let me keep it real: if your current addiction path is trashing major areas of your life, even threatening to end it, then I wouldn't waste energy on labels. You know deep down that things can't stay this way. Whatever you call it, chase after freedom from addiction like your life depends on it—because it truly does.

At a minimum, your relationships (including your marriage), career, and mental, physical, and spiritual health hang by a thread based on whether you can turn this ship around. So, let other people fight over terminology and technicalities. A drowning person doesn't pause to debate whether to call a floatie device a life ring, a lifebuoy, or a lifesaver. When sinking in deep waters, you grab whatever keeps you afloat with both hands and hold on tight.

In the same way, cling with hope to any pathway offering you a way out of addiction's riptide. Stop focusing on questions that don't change the reality of your situation. Instead, fight for your future. Run toward help and don't look back. Surround yourself with support to walk on water again instead of drowning silently.

At the end of the day, call it what you want—recovery, sobriety, or freedom. The name means nothing if the transformation isn't real. Your marriage, family, community, and own soul long to see the person you were created to become before addiction set in. Believe that better and brighter version of yourself waits on the other side of healing. That belief makes all the difference.

I'd also encourage you not to get tangled in endless quibbling over which recovery programs or protocols seem "superior," especially when you're early in the healing process. Some people hype up 12-step communities like Alcoholics Anonymous (AA) or Narcotics Anonymous (NA) as the gold standard. Others prioritize different support groups for personal reasons, whether theological, philosophical, or otherwise. There's no shortage of opinions, that's for sure!

I once had a friend getting into fitness who checked out all these trendy workout regimens and diets. After a while, he laughed and admitted the "best program" he discovered was ... wait for it ... the one he actually committed to doing!

The same principle applies to overcoming addiction. At the end of the day, the "best program" is the one you dive into with grit, authenticity, and consistency—whatever tools help you rewrite your story. So, if something is resonating and you notice your life improving, lean all the way in.

This book may not explicitly align with 12-step language in every instance, but the core principles can strengthen your sobriety regardless of your chosen programs. Remember, the goal is forward progress, not performance. Twelve-step support groups helped save my life, but I know plenty of people who found healing through other means too. What's the bottom line? Ditch the debating and get busy doing. The program itself means nothing if the heart change isn't real. So, stay humble and hopeful; your hardest days are paving your road back home.

The Necessity of Community

Surround yourself with empathy, stick with communities that keep you anchored in truth, and fight for your future. We weren't designed to beat challenges solo. You need a crew of supporters to help you walk steadily toward freedom together. Recovery works best surrounded by diverse perspectives from people focused on your growth:

- **Counselors**—Professionals can equip you to diagnose core issues that keep fueling addiction and help you find workable solutions.
- **Sponsors**—These are individuals who have lived experience. They can offer candid accountability to keep you on track.
- **Peer Support Groups**—12-step meetings or other addiction support groups allow you to share your burdens without shame so you can find encouragement.
- **Caring Friends and Family**—These are people close to you who know your story. They will give encouragement and cheer you on from the sidelines.

Having a wide range of people who give help and support will prevent you from feeling rudderless and alone. Their wisdom can help silence addiction's lies that are saying, *You're hopeless! Just give up trying to quit!* If you buy into that deception, then backsliding is inevitable. Don't let shame trap you in secrecy or isolation any longer.

Lasting change rarely happens in isolation. Instead, it comes from showing up honestly among people who will give you grace when shame feels paralyzing and hold you accountable when necessary. Staying trapped alone in pain breeds secrecy while consistent accountability leads to growth even when you fail.

So, reach out rather than trying to hide. Ask someone you trust to stand by your side when you feel desperate and tempted to make bad choices again. Allow them to redirect you in a loving way. Let them celebrate you when you take baby steps forward. With their encouragement, you can begin envisioning the person you were created to become.

Healing happens slowly but very surely when we stop resisting help. If you currently feel too exhausted or afraid to take the next step, ask someone to carry hope for you. Let them reassure you that with loving support and supernatural strength, you can finish the journey toward freedom. There are warriors waiting to cheer you on if you will have the courage to reach out your hand and accept help. So, muster up courage, get some grit, and let's get going. I'll walk with you in this book, and others are willing to walk with you too. We'll make it through together.

A Question of Faith

What role does faith play in getting sober? There's no one-size-fits-all answer. Let me tell you about my experience, and maybe it'll help you sort out your own thoughts. I'll share more of my addiction story later, but for now, here's part of the faith piece.

I'm a Christian—full transparency. But it wasn't always that way. When my life totally imploded from addiction, I realized I couldn't recover using willpower alone. After too many brushes with death and the law, I finally went to court-ordered rehab. That's where I learned the principles I share here. But real talk? I was sober for over a year before fully embracing Christianity.

Could I maintain sobriety pre-faith? Yes, to an extent. Admitting powerlessness was huge for me. But over time I felt I needed something more significant. Accepting Christ made a big difference in my recovery journey.

Here's an analogy: I had a friend who bought a self-propelled lawnmower but didn't use the self-propel feature. He manually pushed it, making mowing way harder than necessary. I showed him how to engage the self-propel lever, and it was a total game changer.

Recovery without faith is possible. Millions do it. But for me, faith empowered my sobriety in pivotal ways. I'd never judge someone else's personal journey, nor would I hide my own. Speaking the truth as I know it, faith took my recovery to the next level.

My faith is evident in this book, but I didn't want to over-quote Bible verses or risk turning people off. So, even if you're not religious or ready to explore spirituality, please keep reading. My goal is to help you recover and heal relationships damaged by addiction, especially your relationship as a married couple. If I accomplish that, we will have traveled a good, long way together. Your faith journey is between you and God. I hope you will get to know Him, but let's work toward healing either way.

1

HELP! MY SPOUSE IS AN ADDICT!

What You Need to Know About Addiction

As we begin our time together, I want to speak first to the supporting spouse. If you are the spouse who is struggling with an addiction, read along with us. We want to develop a pattern of removing secrets from your relationship, so it's critical for both of you to understand one another's perspective. You are reading this book because one of you is wrestling with an addiction while the other is trying to figure out how to deal with it. So, don't skip anything. Both of you need this information.

When addiction crashes your marriage, everything turns upside down. One day, you and your partner seem solid; the next, you're in complete chaos. All of us have unique personalities, but when you add substances or other forms of addiction, you'll feel like you're living with two or more different people. Your spouse might be fine one day, but then they're distant, moody, and unreliable the next. You start asking yourself, *Just who is this person who lives with me?* Over time, things really begin to seem hopeless, and recovery seems to be a million miles away.

The first thing you should know is your spouse's erratic behavior isn't about you—their brain is lit up and flashing like airport runway lights thanks to substances or addictive behaviors. They keep chasing the lights, trying to come in for a landing, but the runway keeps shifting and their good feelings fade fast until they ultimately nosedive and crash.

It's a sad day when you realize your spouse would rather chase a high than be in a healthy, sober relationship with you. They may genuinely, deeply love you, but something else has gotten in the way. You miss the person you once fell in love with. You'd do anything to get them back. Nagging never works, though, and enabling is even worse. You can't think your way out of this one, and neither can your spouse. Their brain already has been hijacked.

So, is there anything that can be done about the predicament you're in? First, educate yourself. Learn what drives addiction and how it rewires the brain. Why does it take hold, and what does it do to your spouse's brain? How does addiction affect relationships? Even more important: Is there any way to break free from its grasp? Second, focus on your own health and find support. It won't help you to overanalyze your spouse's every mood and action. That's a mental merry-go-round that will keep you spinning and take you nowhere.

Recovery is possible, but it requires commitment from your partner. If they are willing to go "all in" on recovery, your relationship can heal. As for you, be patient but set boundaries. Don't enable bad habits or make excuses for them. Stay hopeful but be real—the road is long and not very straight. Relapse happens. But with hard work, open communication, and self-care, you can rebuild trust and intimacy in your marriage. Your love is stronger than any disease. Refuse to go down with the ship.

Let's start by exploring some information about the nature of addiction. Why do addictions take hold? What do they do to the brain? How do they affect relationships? And most importantly, how can couples break free from them?

You may already know a lot about addiction. If that's the case, consider this chapter a refresher course. If you are new to all this, spend some time learning what drives addiction and what its harmful consequences are. Discover how you can support each other as you pursue sobriety, reconciliation, and personal growth together.

So ... What Is Addiction?

Addiction is when you can't stop a behavior, even when it messes up your life. Another word to describe this kind of behavior is *compulsive.* The brain gets hooked on the good feelings that certain substances or behaviors provide and keeps wanting more.

Here's the science: addictive substances and certain kinds of behavior flood the brain with feel-good chemicals like dopamine. It's a rush at first, but this rush fades fast, so the brain reduces its natural dopamine to compensate. That's what experts mean when they say addiction rewires the brain. The natural supply of dopamine dwindles even while the brain screams out, *More!*

Addiction also hijacks the brain's reward system—the part that makes food, sleep, and sex feel good. So, even when someone knows a substance or behavior is harmful, it's really hard for them to stop. The logic center fights the person's primal instincts. The more they use the substance or engage in the behavior, the more their brain keeps changing to compensate. More leads to "More and more!" Since the brain no longer operates normally, the person needs the substance or the behavior just to feel halfway normal. Like I said, the brain is now lit up like an airport runway. The plane has been hijacked, a crash is coming, and it could be fatal.

Addictions can happen to anyone, but some people are more prone to them if they already struggle with anxiety, depression, or trauma. In fact, geneticists have identified certain DNA patterns that signify someone might be in more danger of addiction. Getting high or engaging in some other kind of behavior numbs the pain, so they'll keep on chasing that quick fix. If you have ever discovered this for yourself by having your DNA analyzed, then, by all means, take it seriously.

The key to understanding addiction is recognizing it as a disease, not a choice. Now, I should qualify that statement—yes, at some point they did choose to take a substance or carry out a certain behavior, but over time their ability to choose all but disappeared. People don't generally decide to become addicted. Certain brains are just more vulnerable, especially if life already feels out of control. At the point addiction takes over, logic also gets hijacked. The person may know that continuing what they're doing is harmful, but their brain says to do it anyway.

I would encourage you as the supporting spouse—and this may be really difficult—to have compassion for the struggle. Create safe spaces for honest talk without shame. Support healthy coping skills. You can't force someone to heal, but you can walk with them on the journey. Recovery takes work, but it is possible.

When people hear the word *addiction,* drugs and alcohol are probably the first things that pop into their minds. However, addiction can happen with anything that hijacks the brain's reward system. If a behavior goes from a habit to a compulsion to an obsession, then it's probably an addiction.

We also hear the word *addict,* and we may only think about hardcore stuff like meth or heroin. But—and this is important to understand—the brain really can't judge. A lot of substances and behaviors can become addictive. Alcohol, pills, and even shopping and pornography use are addictive for some people.

Two Categories of Addiction

Anything that gives the brain that rush of dopamine can lead to an addiction that cries out, *More and more!* When someone gets to that point and tries to stop, they're overwhelmed by anxiety, irritability, and depression. Their brain is staging a major protest, demanding one more hit or whatever gave it the original good feeling.

A person who is using substances or engaging in compulsive behaviors may not like the term *addiction*, but if it's interfering with their health, work, money, or relationships, it's addictive behavior. If they feel like what they're doing is an obligation, then it's an addiction.

When I say almost any substance or behavior can become an addiction, I want to distinguish between two types of addiction. You may be wondering what the difference is between something like a drug addiction versus a food addiction. There are two major categories for addictions: **substance abuse addictions and process addictions.**[1]

Substance Addictions vs. Process Addictions

Addiction can refer to drugs and alcohol, but the brain can get hooked on behaviors too. These behaviors are called process addictions. Common process addictions include gambling, excessive gaming or internet usage, compulsive shopping or spending, sexual addiction, pornography addiction, and even exercise addiction. If it gives someone a rush that they can't stop even when it's unhealthy, it's probably an addiction.

Substance addiction is exactly what it sounds like. A person has used a substance, such as alcohol or a drug, and continued use feels like an obligation. Some substances are more addictive than others, but the results are the same—the brain has been rewired to demand more of the substance.

What's the Difference?

Substance addictions and process addictions both hijack your brain's reward system, but they can impact your body and life differently.

With substances, you can experience physical withdrawal if you try to quit. Think: shakes, sweats, nausea, or other physical symptoms. Your heart rate might go wild. You can have weird episodes of mental confusion or intense body pains depending on what you've been using.

But process addictions, such as pornography use or compulsive spending, don't put foreign chemicals into your body's system. So, there are no physical symptoms if you stop. The impact will be on your mood and behavior.

Substance addictions are often easier to identify. You put substances in your body, while most process addictions are outside the body. Think about it this way: you don't need substances like drugs and alcohol to survive or to be authentically human. Process addictions are different because they are the use or misuse of something humans need to survive and thrive. Here are some examples:

- You need food, but you don't need eight double cheeseburgers in a single meal.
- You need money to survive in modern culture, but you don't need $200 worth of lottery tickets.
- You have an urge to have sex because of the biological imperative to procreate, but you don't need to have sex with every person who is available and willing.

Since you can use money, eat food, and engage in sex in healthy ways, addictions in those areas are harder to identify. So, how do you know when their misuse has become an addiction? Ask yourself these questions:

- Do I have a hard time focusing at school, at work, or with my spouse because I'm itching to game, scroll, or visit a pornography website?
- Do I ignore my spouse because I want to stay online, shop, or gamble?
- Do I have no desire to do anything besides this behavior?
- Is my whole life starting to revolve around this behavior?
- Is my spouse, my boss, or a friend telling me that this behavior is a problem?

There's a second important difference between process and substance addictions: people view them differently. Substance abusers are often told they're making a "choice" to use. People think they deserve the struggles because they "chose" the substance, which means they're subject to some harsh judgment rather than compassion. Meanwhile, process addicts like gamblers, compulsive shoppers, or pornography addicts are often told their addiction "isn't real." Even medical professionals sometimes dismiss their concerns or don't take them seriously.

Finally, treatment is different. Substance abusers usually need medical and psychological help to detox safely. A doctor also needs to check for permanent damage to their body. But process addictions can't be totally eliminated. You can't decide to just stop eating! So, treatment usually focuses more on managing those things in a healthy way.

Both substance and process addictions mess with the brain's chemistry. But substances also tax the body, while process addictions mainly harm relationships, work or school performance, and emotional health. The brain can get hijacked whether a substance or a behavior is involved. The main difference is physical versus psychological dependence. Substances create chemical hooks; behaviors create mental compulsions. Both can take over someone's life.

Addiction is addiction, no matter the type. Compassion and treatment, not judgment, help people heal. Everyone deserves support and a chance at recovery. The good news is that recovery is 100% possible either way.

A List of Addictions

The following list of addictions isn't comprehensive, but these are some of the major addictions people struggle to overcome:

- **Drug Addiction**
  Illegal or prescription medications give a high by activating the brain's reward center. Chasing that dopamine rush can wreck a person's health, relationships, and life.

- **Alcohol Addiction**
  Heavy drinking rewires the brain's neural pathways over time. A person starts craving the alcohol and eventually needs more and more to feel a buzz, thereby damaging the brain. Hangovers become the norm.

- **Gambling Addiction**
  Compulsive gambling gives the brain big chemical thrills. Over time, though, most gamblers lose more than money—relationships, career goals, and trust all start to crumble.

- **Sex Addiction**
  Viewing pornography, engaging in casual hookups, and soliciting sex workers become obsessions because of the dopamine rush they bring. There are quick "highs," but intimacy suffers big time.

- **Food Addiction**
  This includes emotional overeating, binges, and addiction to certain foods. We all crave comfort food sometimes, but relying on food for mood regulation messes up a person's health and self-image.

- **Shopping Addiction**
  Buying things compulsively offers short-term euphoria through a dopamine release, but the emotional and financial toll builds over time, leading to secrecy or deceit.

- **Gaming and Internet Addiction**
  Leveling up, earning likes, and getting followers all signal a dopamine rush to the brain, and those become an addiction when real-life duties and relationships start taking a back seat.

Regardless of the kind of addiction, the cycle is always the same—a quick high followed by a brutal low, even while consequences pile up. Pleasure gives way to pain, and the cycle repeats over and over. I know having a spouse with an addiction can tank your relationship fast. In fact, I know it personally.

Recovery Is Possible

As the supporting spouse, you may feel alone and hopeless. The addicted spouse becomes unavailable to meet your needs. They lash out when confronted. Lies shatter trust. Your relationship orbits around their addiction. It helps to understand that addiction literally rewires the brain's pathways. Their brain is flooded with more feel-good chemicals from substances than even from you. It's not about love. Their brain has been hijacked.

So, as hard as it is to accept, don't take it personally. Your spouse isn't consciously choosing addiction over you. They need healing, and recovery is possible with commitment.

Here are some ways you can keep going while you encourage them to get help and make positive changes:

- Educate yourself on their addiction so you can empathize.
- Set clear boundaries and stop enabling behaviors.
- Get counseling and join support groups for yourself to address underlying factors like trauma, depression, and insecurity.
- Prioritize self-care and your own mental health.
- Be patient but stand firm if they relapse or lie.
- Believe in their ability to regain control of their life.
- Stay hopeful. With compassion, trust, and hard work, your relationship can heal.
- Remove triggers. Get rid of any substances or temptations to engage in addictive behaviors at home. Avoid people and places that could lead to backsliding.
- Fill your time with good stuff. Help replace addictive habits with new hobbies, interests, and healthy activities. Follow your passions like art, sports, or volunteering.
- Rebuild intimacy. Have real talk about the damage done. Express hurt feelings but also offer forgiveness. Nurture emotional and physical closeness in healthy ways.
- Get couple's counseling. Work with a therapist who specializes in addiction and relationships. Develop tools for communicating needs, resolving conflict, and building trust.
- Mark progress. Celebrate periods of sobriety and growth through meaningful rituals and experiences together that affirm how far your spouse has come.

Healing is tough, but you've got this. With perseverance and faith in each other, your relationship will emerge stronger. Each victory is proof you can recreate what you had and more. Understanding addiction is your first step.

When addiction is in your relationship, emotions can go wild. Your words hold a lot of power. What you say matters, but *how* you say it matters even more. Speak with compassion, not judgment or anger. Choose words that uplift and motivate, not accuse or shame. Be real with, yet in control of, your emotions. Listen with patience. Create openness. Avoid lecturing or demanding. Convey hope, empathy, and unwavering support.

Harsh vibes feed shame and will push your spouse away. Tread carefully; speak lovingly. Your tone can make the difference between isolation and openness, resistance and cooperation, and despair and determination.

Words can wound, or they can heal. Pay attention to both *what* and *how* you speak. You've got this!

Personal Reflection

Answer the following questions:

1. What addictive behaviors or substances am I or my spouse struggling with right now? How are they impacting my health and relationships?

   _____

   _____

   _____

2. Do I truly believe recovery is possible? What fears hold me back from committing fully to the process that will lead to sobriety? What fears do I have about my spouse's commitment?

   _____

   _____

   _____

3. What new hobbies, interests, or healthy activities can I pursue for my personal growth and healing?

_____

_____

_____

4. How can I rebuild intimacy and trust with my spouse after the damage that addiction has done to our relationship? What do I need from my spouse?

_____

_____

_____

5. What triggers me or my spouse back into addictive behaviors, and how can we remove them from our lives?

_____

_____

_____

6. Am I being honest with myself and my spouse about the pain and damage addiction has caused? What secrets am I still keeping?

_____

_____

_____

7. How is addiction impacting my mood, reliability, and emotional availability?

_____

_____

_____

8. How will I celebrate victories and track the progress toward sobriety? What meaningful rituals can mark new beginnings?

_____

_____

_____

Couple's Discussion

Discuss the following with your spouse:

1. How has addiction disrupted trust and intimacy in our marriage? How can we start rebuilding our relationship?
2. What forms of counseling or support groups would benefit our marriage as we cope with this challenge?
3. How can we better support each other through the ups and downs of recovery and avoid hurtful accusations?
4. What boundaries need to be in place to prevent enabling and to protect the health of our relationship?
5. How will we recognize genuine progress and celebrate victories together along the recovery journey?
6. What emotional work is needed to move beyond bitterness and offer forgiveness?
7. How can we create openness for honest conversations without judgment or shame?
8. What new shared interests or activities can we pursue to fill time constructively?
9. How can we increase our emotional and physical intimacy in healthy ways as our relationship heals?
10. What words of encouragement would be meaningful to hear from each other right now?

NOTES

2

TALK TO ME

Getting Communication Back in Order

Now that we've learned some things about how addiction works, I want to move to another topic that will help you get your relationship back on track: *communication*. Some of what I will say applies to the supporting spouse, some to the addicted spouse, and some to both of you. Again, I encourage you to read all of it, as it will help you communicate with and understand each other better.

Relationships are hard. I would be lying if I told you anything different. All marriages have difficulties, not just the ones that are dealing with an addiction. So, in case no one has told you: if you want to have a healthy marriage, then it's going to take a lot of work. *A lot.* There are going to be struggles. But I'm also telling you that if you work through those difficult times together, your bond can become unbreakable.

Steering Through the Storm

Have you ever seen a movie about a ship or a fishing boat in the middle of a storm? I can think of at least a half dozen off the top of my head. You mostly know the plot before you even sit down to watch it. The weather and other unfavorable conditions are going to batter that boat until it finally sinks. The entire movie is about the struggle before the inevitable conclusion. You're sad when you realize the situation is hopeless, but you're also sort of relieved when it's finally over. Now the survivors can accept the tragedy and try to move on.

When addiction rears its ugly head in a marriage, it's like that boat in the storm. The deceit required to hide an addiction destroys openness and trust, leading to a massive breakdown in communication. Addicts tend to avoid taking responsibility for their actions, and discussions shift to their partners' faults instead. Meanwhile, a supporting spouse grows resentful and contemptuous. Defensiveness swells on both sides. As far as anyone can tell, the ship is going down. It's just a matter of time, and the survivors will be left to pick up the pieces.

At the point communication breaks down, the couple loses the friendship and fun that once colored their interactions. They stop having real, vulnerable conversations. Talking turns into disconnected monologues, like two people speaking on top of each other about their own stuff. There's no actual listening or connecting anymore. This communication breakdown leaves both spouses feeling unheard and misunderstood. The damage seems impossible to repair. Looking from the outside, we watch as the ship starts to go under. How can the marriage possibly stay afloat?

What You Must Do to Stay Afloat

Let's start with first things first. Continuing the analogy of a ship in a storm, you have to plug the leaks in the boat before you can navigate back to dry land. You will need to learn new communication skills to navigate in your marriage together, but for the moment, just stop making things worse—plug the leaks. Stabilize your relationship and right the ship. Make the choice to communicate differently. Recovery begins as you change the way you speak to each other. Here are five communication skills to work on while you stabilize your relationship:

1. **Begin by speaking gently, with care and without accusation.** Choose words that convey hope rather than shame. Uplifting communication makes sobriety feel possible. Harshness only pushes the addicted spouse away and drives the supporting spouse to despair. Shouting, pouting, manipulating, and name-calling have no place in a loving relationship, so if you're doing any of those, just stop! Meet each other with empathy, not judgment. If you're trying to overcome addiction, your spouse is concerned, hurt, and probably angry—and with good cause. Avoid hurtful words to each other. Don't wait until tomorrow to change the way you talk. Start today!

2. **Listen deeply before responding.** Ask thoughtful questions to understand your spouse's struggles. Openly share your own heart. Honesty lays the groundwork for trust and reconciliation.

3. **Inject friendship and fun into your interactions.** Laugh, be playful, and make new memories. Eliminate sarcasm and hurtful humor. Joy and friendship will rebuild the foundation for your partnership. Share encouragement and appreciation to restore the intimacy you once had. Love can conquer addiction, and it begins by treating your spouse like a friend you care about deeply.

4. **Develop your conflict resolution skills.** As tensions start rising, take a break to cool off. Then return to the discussion calmly. Don't use a break as an excuse for stonewalling. The purpose of cooling off is to manage your emotions, not to ignore each other.

5. **Surround yourselves with positive influences.** It will help you to find other couples who have struggled with similar issues and found a way out of the crisis. Seek counseling, support groups, church friends, and other people who will lift you up as a couple. Don't let shame cause you to isolate. You need community, encouragement, and practical help. With faith, perseverance, and a team of friends by your side, you will get through this.

Start with the most important thing in your communication as a couple: *stop the bleeding!* Plug the leak. Quit making thing worse. If you can't do it on your own, get someone to help you. Toxic communication needs to end today.

Making Your Spouse Your Priority

Once you stop the type of communication that is damaging your relationship, the next thing to do is get your head on straight about your priorities. I'm a Christian, so my top priority is God, but after that, my spouse is my priority over anyone or anything else. No other human should take your spouse's place on your priority list. One of the most important ways you show your spouse that they are your top priority is how you communicate with them.

Even marriages untouched by addiction need consistent care and communication. It's not enough to keep telling your spouse they're your number one—you have to show it through dedicated time and presence.

As you begin restoring and improving communication with your spouse, try setting aside at least 30–60 uninterrupted minutes with your spouse every day. Remove distractions and give them your full attention. Go on walks, free from electronics and multitasking. Actively listen and ask thoughtful questions. Share your hearts, dreams, and struggles. Build up your love daily through this one-on-one time. This is one of the most meaningful ways to show your spouse that they are your number one priority.

Here are some additional ways to communicate that will show your spouse they are your top priority:

- Get away as just the two of you several days per year. Dream together about your future. Talk about your short-term goals and long-term aspirations. Brainstorm action plans and consider the steps you'll take as a team. Align your vision to prevent issues from arising later on.

- Fill up your partner's "love tank" through affection, praise, and encouragement. Flirt, send sweet texts, and reminisce over memories. Keep your romance alive. A strong friendship will sustain your partnership.

- When conflict inevitably comes, handle it calmly. Don't attack your spouse's character. Instead, discuss how specific actions make you feel and be sure to take ownership of your own shortcomings too. Seek compromise. Forgive quickly and move forward in peace.

- Surround your marriage with uplifting influences such as positive friends, marriage enrichment events, and couples you admire. Guard against toxic people and media. Protect your union from outside interference. Join support groups and pursue counseling. Surround yourselves with good mentors. You do not have to walk this road alone.

- Set healthy boundaries around technology and hobbies, never choosing screens over face-to-face interaction. Prioritize relationship-building activities over distractions. Your spouse deserves your best. Remember, they're your number one.

- When offenses happen, apologize sincerely and seek forgiveness. Then take steps to rebuild trust through changed behavior over time. Do your best to repair hurts quickly before they deepen.

- Accept your partner as they are, embracing their uniqueness. Don't criticize their personality or try to force them to conform to your image. Celebrate your differences and learn from each other.

- No matter how long you have been together, keep dating! Plan fun outings, try new hobbies, go on adventures, and be silly and affectionate.

- Make intimacy a priority by protecting time for physical connection as well as emotional availability. Sex helps couples feel close and cherished.

- Pray together for unity, healing of past wounds, and fulfillment of your shared purpose. Seek wisdom and strength from above.

It takes work to build a strong relationship that can handle anything life throws your way. It won't happen on its own. You've got to put in consistent effort and be brave enough to open up and let your guard down. Share your real feelings, struggles, and dreams. That vulnerability creates huge levels of trust and connection. Keep your spouse as your number one in all the ways you interact with each other. It will go a long way in repairing and strengthening your marriage.

Tips to Build Your Communication Muscles

Communication seems to be an area of struggle for all couples. Yes, some do better than others, but communication difficulties in marriages are pretty universal. If I could solve all your communication issues as a couple in a single chapter, I would have already sold it and retired! Even though this chapter won't solve all your problems with communication, it is a good start. I want to give you some additional tips to help you build your communication muscles. As I mentioned before, it won't always be easy—you're going to have to work at it.

When someone you love is battling an addiction, emotions tend to explode. As a supporting spouse, you might experience frustration, resentment, and loneliness. It's like a roller coaster without the thrill. You may experience all the pain of lies and betrayal, but lashing out won't help. You've got to find it within yourself to act beyond your feelings. Yes, hurting people hurt people, but that doesn't mean you're required to return pain for pain. You can do something different.

The words we use carry immense power. They can either build our loved ones up or tear them down. When you want to improve your communication, be as intentional with how you speak as what you say. Season your speech with compassion.

These tips will help you improve and grow your communication muscles:

- **The tone behind your words matters most.** Speak gently, not to accuse but to encourage. Words can either push your partner away in shame or draw them close with hope. This goes for both people—the spouse struggling with addiction and the spouse who is trying to walk through it with them.
- **Do your best to listen without interrupting.** Ask real questions. Share your heart. Open up about your own struggles too—we've all got them. Vulnerability builds trust and intimacy.
- **Listen fully before formulating a response.** Reflect back what you heard. Seek clarification. Empathetic listening creates openness and understanding. Don't listen to respond—listen to understand.
- **Use "I feel" statements rather than "you" accusations.** When sharing emotional topics or complaints, take ownership of your own perspective. Avoid attacking your spouse's character. Criticism provokes defensiveness and shuts down communication. Share your heart genuinely but without judgment.
- **Make your partner feel heard and known by asking thoughtful questions.** Dig deep to understand their experiences, beliefs, dreams, and fears. Don't stay surface-level. Create an atmosphere where vulnerability is safe.

- **Understand that there will be setbacks because recovery isn't linear.** Even in 12-step groups, everyone knows that sometimes a step must be repeated. Give grace when an addicted spouse slips up and keep believing in their ability to change. You will find that your faith may be the one thing that lifts them up when nothing else will.
- **Attack the problem, not each other.** You have a common enemy in dealing with addiction, but it's not your spouse. Complaints aired gently in the right context build intimacy because they prevent small issues from becoming bigger.
- **Offer sincere encouragement, praise, and expressions of appreciation.** Let your spouse know the qualities you respect and value in them. Affirmation strengthens your bond.
- **Combine truth with love, not anger or ego.** Approach conflict resolution not as enemies but as teammates. Seek compromise. Be quick to forgive and don't keep score.
- **Pray together for strength and unity.** I strongly believe God's power can restore your relationship.
- **Get outside help if needed.** Find a good counselor. Attend workshops and groups. You need to know you're not alone in your struggle, so surround yourselves with positive people who will cheer you on.

The Thrill of Changing Together

Real relationships aren't social media perfect. They take work! Let your spouse fully in, past the filters. Yes, you'll annoy each other sometimes even if addiction isn't a problem in your relationship anymore. It happens. Learn to apologize quickly and let it go. Those bumps can actually bring you closer as you choose love over pride. Accept each other's quirks. Have each other's backs.

Make your relationship your top priority. When times get tough, cling tightly to each other and to faith. Work through it together. The messier the story, the more epic the love. Stay hopeful because the final chapter is still unwritten. Your loyalty and teamwork will shine. Write an adventure worth reading.

Personal Reflection

Answer the following questions:

1. How can I improve the way I communicate with my spouse, especially when tensions are high?

   _____

   _____

   _____

2. Am I speaking to my spouse with gentleness, empathy, and care right now? If not, what needs to change?

   _____

   _____

   _____

3. What are some ways I can show my spouse through my words and actions that they are my top priority?

   _____

   _____

   _____

4. Do I make time every day for quality, uninterrupted communication with my spouse? If not, how can I start building this habit?

   _____

   _____

   _____

5. Am I fully present when my spouse is speaking to me, or am I distracted? How would my spouse answer this about me? How can I become a better listener?

_____

_____

_____

6. Do I ask thoughtful questions to really understand my spouse's inner world? How can I create an atmosphere of safety for vulnerability?

_____

_____

_____

7. How well do I handle conflict? Do I attack the problem or my spouse? How can I learn to fight fair?

_____

_____

_____

8. Do I apologize quickly when I mess up? How can I get better at sincerely saying "I'm sorry" and making amends?

_____

_____

_____

Couple's Discussion Questions

Discuss the following with your spouse:

1. What are some ways we can improve our communication, especially when we're feeling hurt or angry? How can we speak gently and listen fully?

2. Do we make time every day to really connect and talk openly, without distractions? If not, how can we start building this habit together?

3. Are there any ongoing sources of conflict we keep clashing over? How can we attack the problem, not each other, and seek compromise?

4. Do we feel truly heard, known, and understood by each other? If not, what steps can we take to build more empathy and vulnerability?

5. How would we rate the health of our friendship and fun right now? What activities or rituals can we establish to keep our romance and laughter alive?

6. Do we need to apologize to each other for any hurts? How can we get better at sincerely saying "I'm sorry" and making amends when we mess up?

7. What boundaries or habits do we need to set around technology and other distractions to make more time for each other?

8. Are we fully open with each other? What fears or struggles are we tempted to hide from each other? How can we create more safety?

9. Do we affirm each other enough through words of encouragement, praise, and appreciation? How can we get better at this?

10. Do we need to surround ourselves with more positive influences, mentors, or counselors? Whom can we reach out to for support and growth?

NOTES

3

FINDING RHYTHM IN RECOVERY

Self-Focus Without Being Selfish

In this chapter, I want to begin first by talking to the addicted spouse about the recovery process itself. You may have heard that you should be "selfish" in recovery. While you must focus on yourself as you pursue sobriety, you are still married. Selfishness never works well in a marriage, yet you have to be focused and diligent about the recovery process. You will need rhythm and balance to seek sobriety while maintaining a healthy relationship with your partner. What does this look like in real life? Here's a window into the lives of Vincent and Grace, a hypothetical married couple who faced the dilemma of finding balance in recovery.

Vincent and Grace's Journey

When Vincent first started on the road to recovery, he zeroed in on staying sober. He poured himself into daily recovery meetings, connected with a sponsor, started therapy, and read "quit lit" books that shared stories of addiction and sobriety. Grace wanted to be supportive. She made them dinner before his group sessions and avoided triggers like alcohol and unmonitored prescription medications in their apartment. She knew focusing inward would help Vincent establish his sobriety.

Nevertheless, weeks passed and Vincent was rarely available, emotionally or physically. He was either at meetings or withdrawn, glued to recovery TikTok videos and other addiction-related websites. When she asked him to make time for their standing weekly date nights, Vincent became defensive. He even went so far as to accuse her of undermining his recovery. Grace allowed resentment to fester, and she started to refer to herself as a "sobriety widow."

Things came to a head when Vincent disappeared on a three-day retreat for recovering addicts—something he decided to attend at the last minute without consulting Grace. She felt as though her needs weren't even an afterthought. When Vincent returned, Grace calmly but directly said his extreme self-focus had crossed over into hurtful selfishness. She reminded him that she wanted to support his sobriety, but he needed to uphold his role in their marriage, too.

Chastened, Vincent apologized for neglecting Grace's needs. Inspired by a marriage enrichment book, he agreed to weekly check-ins with Grace to ask whether he was balancing his recovery with caring for his marriage. He began to discuss meetings and therapy progress openly with Grace instead of keeping her in the dark. One of the most meaningful things he did was commit to bimonthly date nights focused completely on quality time together with Grace—no distractions. Knowing that self-work fortified Vincent's sobriety, Grace was motivated to be patient during the weeks when Vincent's recovery work was especially heavy.

The couple weathered ups and downs, but they slowly found their rhythm. Grace joined Vincent at a sobriety workshop focused on spouses reconnecting intimately. He celebrated Grace's big promotion at work by planning a weekend spa retreat. Little by little, they nurtured trust and friendship in the midst of the recovery lifestyle. Vincent maintained his nonnegotiable meetings while assuring Grace she was his top priority outside of fixed recovery commitments. When Grace herself struggled with body image, Vincent returned the patience and compassion she had given to him.

Over the years, they discovered that brutal period of finding balance made them a stronger couple as they cemented skills like communication, vulnerability, and forgiveness. Today, Vincent's sobriety remains steady, and he now sponsors others battling addiction and isolation. Above all, his journey taught him and Grace that defeating addiction is a team effort; it can only be maintained through considering your partner an equal player in healing. Together, they stand as proof that finding rhythm makes a marriage stronger than ever.

Your Recovery and Your Relationship

Do the experiences of Vincent and Grace sound familiar? To begin pursuing sobriety, it's crucial to devote some serious energy to the process. Detoxing, managing cravings, finding a support group—all those steps have to be a priority. But that necessary focus on self-care can sometimes spill over into thinking only about yourself while ignoring your partner's needs.

How can you walk the line between being selfish versus taking care of yourself and being a good marriage partner? I know it's tricky, but it's also totally doable. In this chapter, I want to share some tips to help the two of you collaborate on a plan so you can get some "me time" to work on your recovery while still showing up for your relationship with your partner.

Why You Need "Me Time"

Early in recovery, directing your energy inwardly and on yourself helps you:

- Safely withdraw and handle painful detox.
- Go to intensive treatment and counseling.
- Work closely with your sponsor for accountability.
- Avoid tempting people and places tied to your addiction.
- Build healthy new routines and coping strategies.
- Process underlying issues connected to your addiction in therapy.
- Create social support networks in recovery communities.
- Make amends, when possible, to those hurt by your addiction.

This self-focus lays the foundation for you to get and stay sober. Recovery is hard, personal work that no one else can do for you. You have to make big lifestyle changes yourself. That is the reason why you will need to put yourself first sometimes to get well. In fact, your spouse needs you to put in the effort it takes to recover.

How Self-Care Can Become Selfishness

Self-care takes effort, but being constantly self-absorbed always backfires. You have to stay *self-aware* so your recovery focus doesn't slip into selfishness that ignores your partner. Signs you've crossed from reasonable self-care into excessive selfishness include the following:

- Believing your needs are most important, even more than those of your spouse or other family members.
- Ignoring family duties.
- Withdrawing emotionally or physically from your partner.
- Disappearing to recovery activities without informing your spouse.
- Making big decisions that affect your spouse without consulting them first.
- Lashing out when your partner shares their needs.
- Using recovery to justify ongoing secrecy or isolation.

What Is Healthy Self-Care?

None of those behaviors will help you restore or strengthen your marriage. Instead, focus on healthy self-care that facilitates your recovery while also nurturing your marriage. The following are examples of healthy self-care:

- Going to required meetings but also setting aside quality time with your spouse.
- Making reasonable compromises on family duties.
- Staying intimate emotionally and physically with your spouse.
- Communicating transparently about the time needed for recovery.
- Considering your partner's perspective in big decisions.
- Listening to your spouse's needs with empathy.

Discuss healthy balance with your spouse. It will help both of you land on a reasonable solution that will meet both of your needs. Recovery is a priority, but healthy recovery shouldn't overshadow or compromise your relationship.

When Self-Focus Backfires

When self-focus during recovery gets outsized and turns into selfishness, it actively hurts the process in these ways:

- You lose a major support. Recovery is way harder without an understanding partner in your corner.
- Resentment and distance build in your marriage, straining your bond even more.
- It prevents you from learning healthy relationship skills like compromise, vulnerability, and conflict resolution.
- Selfishness stops you from taking accountability for the harm you've caused. However, making amends will help you maintain sobriety.
- Self-absorption itself is addictive and centered on instant gratification. It ultimately undercuts the hard work recovery actually demands.

Healing addiction means you must keep perspective, which includes understanding how your actions impact those who love you. Losing sight of their experiences through selfishness will sabotage your recovery.

Finding Rhythm as a Couple

Here are ways to avoid slipping into selfishness as you take time for self-care in recovery:

- Talk openly about what you need to help you in recovery and give a heads-up whenever possible.
- Schedule dedicated couple time in the middle of recovery stuff to keep intimacy alive.
- Practice balancing a recovery lifestyle with your marriage life.
- Check in on how your spouse is feeling and actively listen with empathy.
- Make amends for harm you have caused by your addiction.
- Consistently follow through on promises.
- Incorporate stress-relief practices for your spouse, too. Support their pursuit of wellness.
- Seek counseling together to get on same page on any sticky relationship issues.
- Clarify your household roles and duties. Renegotiate when necessary.
- Discuss how any big decisions will impact you both before taking action.
- Explore recovery activities you can tackle together, such as couples' therapy.
- Share feelings honestly but calmly. Avoid blame and defensiveness.
- Offer compassion to each other and recognize that recovery is grueling.
- Recognize small selfless acts and ways you both work to repair your relationship. Healing brings more healing.

With compromise and grace, you can balance self-care with nurturing your marriage. Defeat addiction together as a team. Remind yourselves that sobriety allows you to show up fully for each other.

I want to close this chapter with one word of caution. I have written this book with some presuppositions, one of which is that both of you are eagerly seeking recovery. But I also know you may not be reading this book with equal enthusiasm.

Couples are not always on the same page about recovery. Sometimes the supporting spouse can't see the severity of the addiction because it's not their addiction. They may wonder, *Why can't they just stop doing what they're doing so we can get back to "normal"?* or ask, "Why can't I have an occasional glass of wine at home? I'm not the alcoholic!" It could also be that the supporting spouse has been hurt so deeply that they no longer have the energy to encourage their spouse's sobriety. All these feelings are understandable.

To the spouse struggling with addiction: I know those situations can be difficult. Regardless, you must hold tight to your sobriety because your life depends on it. Even if things are not great between you and your spouse right now, don't let that derail your pursuit of sobriety. Your spouse may eventually come to understand just how serious the situation really is, or they may not. Seek sobriety regardless. You may have to continue the process of making amends with your spouse. Don't think you can demand forgiveness immediately. That process can take a long time, and they need to see you have genuinely changed.

If you are the supporting spouse and you can't quite understand the seriousness or severity of your spouse's addiction, or you don't feel you have the energy to keep forgiving and supporting them through the recovery process, please seek support. Recovery isn't easy for anyone involved. Help is available if you will accept it.

Personal Reflection

Answer the following questions:

1. On a scale of 1–10, how would I rate the balance right now between my, or my spouse's, focus on recovery and attention to our marriage? What needs to be adjusted?

_____

_____

_____

2. Have recovery needs been clearly communicated? How can transparency be improved?

_____

_____

_____

3. Has recovery become an excuse to withdraw from intimacy or the needs of our marriage? How can this improve?

_____

_____

_____

4. Do I make decisions unilaterally that affect my partner? How can I include their perspective?

_____

_____

_____

5. Am I practicing empathy when my spouse shares vulnerable feelings? Do I listen well?

_____

_____

_____

6. How can I prioritize bonding time with my spouse amidst a busy recovery schedule? Do we connect enough?

_____

_____

_____

7. Has recovery revealed any lingering marriage issues that we should address in counseling?

_____

_____

_____

Couple's Discussion Questions

Discuss the following with your spouse:

1. How can we make sure recovery gets the focus it needs while still connecting as a couple? What's a reasonable balance?

2. What are the most meaningful ways the supporting spouse could assist in the addicted spouse's recovery journey?

3. How open has the addicted spouse been about the time spent in meetings or recovery activities? How can we improve communication about this?

4. Have I been making unilateral decisions without considering how they affect my spouse? How can we be more considerate of each other?

5. Is the addicted spouse following through consistently on any recovery commitments or promises? Where can there be improvement?

6. How well are we validating each other's feelings and listening when we share openly? Do we respond with empathy?

7. Should we brainstorm new ways to nurture intimacy and friendship amidst the demands of recovery?

8. Are there any self-care or stress-relief techniques that we both could benefit from?

NOTES

4

THE RIGHT GAME ON THE RIGHT PLAYGROUND

People, Spaces, Habits, and Focus

When addiction invades a marriage, it can hollow out the relationship from within, slowly pulling spouses away from each other. To heal the bond, the journey of recovery must involve foundational changes in lifestyle. That means a person struggling with addiction must change their environment and habits as well as any people who facilitated their addictive behavior. To illustrate what I mean, consider the story of Ben.

Ben Gets New Friends

Ben was always a cheerful, kindhearted kid who worked hard in school. He loved playing sports, drawing comics, and helping his parents cook dinner every night. Ben got good grades, and all of his teachers enjoyed having him in class.

However, when Ben started middle school, he met some guys he thought were really "cool." They invited him to go skateboarding with them. Though his parents had warned Ben to avoid troublemakers, he was excited to make new friends. The guys seemed fun—they talked about girls, blasted edgy music, and dared each other to pull pranks like knocking over trash cans and breaking mailboxes.

Ben felt torn. He wanted to fit in but knew his family would disapprove of his rowdy new friends. Before long, Ben started telling small lies to evade questions about where he disappeared to after school. His grades slipped as homework took a backseat to hanging out. Eventually, Ben even got caught shoplifting with his friends one Saturday.

At home, Ben grew sullen and irritable. He often rolled his eyes when his parents asked him to help clean the dishes or walk the dog. Dinner used to be filled with laughter, but now Ben ignored his family in favor of scrolling on his phone. His parents felt him emotionally withdrawing day by day.

One night, the police showed up at Ben's home because he and his friends had been caught spray-painting a highway overpass, and one of the boys had a bag of marijuana in his pocket. All of the boys had to go before a juvenile court judge who sentenced them to a fine and community service. Ben's terrified parents grounded him. They insisted he end the toxic friendships steering him off course.

Of course, readers of this chapter are likely much older than Ben, but you may have had some similar experiences when you were younger. You understand that juveniles sometimes make mistakes that cost them dearly and start them on a road of crime and addiction. Nevertheless, you also recognize the pattern. Peer pressure doesn't disappear as we grow older; it only becomes more sophisticated.

American entrepreneur Jim Rohn once said, "You are the average of the five people you spend the most time with."[1] Rohn may have been thinking about similar words that author Miguel de Cervantes put into the mouth of *Don Quixote's* Sancho Panza: "Tell me your company, and I will tell you what you are."[2] Or the quote may have originated with the New Testament's apostle Paul who said, "Bad company corrupts good character" (1 Corinthians 15:33 NLT). The point is the same: when recovering from addiction, take a hard look at the people in your life—your "crew," so to speak. Also consider your usual activities and surroundings. In this chapter, I want to tell you how to intentionally create a new ecosystem of healthy relationships, environments, and habits that will empower your sobriety and strengthen your marriage.

What Surrounds You?

You've got to assess what current parts of your world might be enabling your addiction.

- **Your People**—Which friends join you when you're using substances or engaging in other addictive behaviors? Who makes excuses for your risky behaviors? Who questions you or tries to sabotage your recovery efforts?
- **Your Spaces**—What bars, parties, or other places stir up cravings connected to your old habits? What homes or neighborhoods kindle patterns of addiction for you?
- **Your Habits**—From sports to hobbies to spending time alone, what activities or even small routines have become strongly linked to your addiction over time?

- **Your Focus**—Has your addiction gradually crowded out the energy you once devoted to family time or passions outside of enabling behaviors?

Take a courageous personal inventory in these four areas. Environments that tempt you and enablers who hold you back or drag you down have got to be dropped from your circle. Halfway measures won't cut it.

Building a Playground That Supports Sobriety

Creating a lifestyle that supports your sobriety should be a team effort between you and your spouse. Uplift and motivate one another toward curating new healthy patterns together. The *four core pillars* for establishing this healed habitat include:

1. **Your Healing Crew**
    - Find fellow support group members or friends in recovery who speak life into your journey.
    - Spend time with other couples and friends practicing sober, intentional living.
    - Look to sponsors, counselors, pastors, and mentors who offer empathy and wisdom from lived experience.
    - Lean on family, community, and church friends who cheer you on through the growth process.

2. **Substance-Free Zones**
    - Avoid places like bars or party scenes that could trigger old habits.
    - Make new positive connections through healthy activities.
    - Volunteer together to contribute at your church or in your local area.
    - Level up your skills for work or passion projects through classes or online instruction.

3. **Intentional Habits**
    - Reignite old passions or uncover new interests that excite you.
    - Develop consistent lifestyle routines, such as proper sleep, nutrition, and exercise.
    - Join recreational groups to replace isolation with belonging.
    - Feed your mind through books, podcasts, documentaries, and courses.
    - Replace toxic habits with adventures that help you feel alive.

4. **Clarified Priorities**
  - Make your marriage your top priority through shared experiences.
  - Reinvest in family connections or commitments that you previously neglected.
  - Embrace self-care practices so you can show up healthily for others.

Let these four pillars guide you as you deliberately embrace new, life-giving routines and social connections. Coauthor the next chapter of your story with your spouse.

Working Together on Your New Playground

Rebuilding your life should be a joint effort with your spouse as you bounce back from addiction. Think back to the passions that used to light you up before substances or other addictive behaviors hijacked your brain. Fan those sparks back into flames. Brainstorm bucket list ideas, new hobbies, or adventures that excite you. Dream big!

Scope out local classes, volunteer groups, recreation teams, and support groups you can join forces with. Surround yourself with healthy people in healthy environments. You may need to delete old contacts from your phone or unfollow triggers on social media. Have honest conversations if certain friendships are getting toxic. Don't let anyone sabotage your growth.

Map out your goals as a couple. These could include races you'll train for, trips you'll take, or skills you'll learn. Develop a common vision together. Lock in regular bonding times like date nights.

Identify uplifting daily rituals that keep you and your partnership solid, like praying, reading, or exercising together. Choose people and activities that leave you feeling peaceful and purposeful. Drop connections that emotionally and spiritually drain you. Protect the oasis you and your spouse are building together.

Learning to Discern in Your New Environment

When stepping into new environments and friendships during your recovery journey, it's important to stay real with yourself by vetting people and situations with discernment. Pay attention to any internal red flags that arise. Does something trigger old urges or cravings? Do these new friends seem to admire qualities you're trying to move away from? Have frequent, open, and ego-free check-ins with your spouse about how new activities or people are making you feel. Do they seem helpful and beneficial, or do they feel risky and dangerous? If you notice any relapse warning signs, halt your involvement immediately rather than looking for reasons to justify going down a harmful path. Your future is what matters most here.

When establishing new connections, focus more on shared values rather than surface-level common history. It doesn't matter if you've known each other since childhood if your old friends are leading you toward destruction. Seek people who value your sobriety rather than merely reconnecting with old buddies from your past. Communicate your recovery story and boundaries in a calm way when you meet potential new friends. The right people will respond with understanding and encouragement rather than judgment. Before revisiting activities that were once tied to substance use or addictive behaviors, evaluate honestly whether you can separate them from the addiction. If you can't, leave them behind without regret. Ask yourself whether your new pursuits actually fill your time constructively long-term versus just distracting or numbing you temporarily. Can you see the difference?

By continually reassessing each new atmosphere you enter, you will keep your recovery environment protected. The bottom line is this: choose to surround yourself with people and places that lead you to health and wholeness.

Growing in Your New Playground

Ultimately, the people and activities you embrace will either help you like water and sunlight help a plant grow, or they will poison and contaminate your progress. Here are some checklists you should consider as you seek new friends and choose new activities:

Find friends who ...

- Have shared interests, values, and worldviews.
- Encourage your personal growth.
- Instill positive mindsets.
- Give a healthy perspectives of life.

Choose activities that ...

- Give you opportunities to expand your capabilities.
- Create social connections to widen your community.
- Encourage physical, emotional, and spiritual health.
- Serve as outlets for fun, adventure, and passion.
- Help you adopt new routines that encourage sobriety.
- Support consistent self-care and feed your soul.

- Provide meaningful family bonding time.
- Build intimacy with your spouse.

By intentionally curating the people you hang out with and the activities you engage in, you fertilize the soil of recovery and relationship growth. Like any garden, the healthier the soil, the stronger the plants. Double down on the choices that give you energy, clarity, and support.

The Gift of a New Playground

Your new playground is a gift. Enjoy it by establishing some protective boundaries. Like kids playing freely on a swing set, it's much better with soft padding underneath. Set wise limits to make sure addiction triggers won't have footholds in your life or marriage. Carefully tend this new habitat, and it will give back to you again and again. Soon the laughter and adventure will return, and your joy will be restored. As you and your spouse stand united in your vision for a good future, take heart. These difficult days will get better as long as you protect the gift of marriage you've been given.

Personal Reflection

Answer the following questions:

1. What parts of my or my spouse's old environments, habits, activities, or friendships are no longer serving us or supporting recovery?

   _____

   _____

   _____

2. What passions, interests, or priorities have I neglected that I want to reinvigorate?

   _____

   _____

   _____

3. What warning signs or red flags tend to precede relapses? How can we catch and halt these patterns earlier?

_____

_____

_____

4. What daily practices or routines give me energy, clarity, purpose, or community connection? How can I incorporate more of these?

_____

_____

_____

5. Who are the people who encourage growth versus endanger progress? How much access are we giving both groups?

_____

_____

_____

6. How can we communicate needs, boundaries, and our recovery story more effectively to old friends or when meeting new people?

_____

_____

_____

7. What goals, adventures, or experiences light me up when I imagine them? How can I take steps toward making them a reality?

_____

_____

_____

8. How am I showing up as a partner in this marriage? Where can I give more support, understanding, or encouragement?

_____

_____

_____

9. What places or environments relax me, inspire me, or make me feel most fully myself? How can I spend more time there?

_____

_____

_____

Couple's Discussion Questions

Discuss the following with your spouse:

1. How can we thoughtfully expand our social circles to include more positive influences?
2. What dreams or goals can we align around to motivate our continued growth together?
3. What home, work, or lifestyle changes would help strengthen our commitment to sobriety and marital unity?
4. How can we lovingly hold each other accountable if we notice warning signs of relapse?
5. What boundaries or protections would help us feel safe from risky people or situations?
6. How are we each taking initiative to nurture our physical, mental, emotional, and spiritual health? Where is there room for growth?
7. What shared interests or passions could we bond over more that energize our marriage?
8. What does a vibrant, adventurous marriage and family look like for us in five years? What about 10 years? How can we align our daily choices toward that vision?

NOTES

5

YOU CAN BE THE "ONE"

Choosing to Be the Exception in Recovery

When I was in school, I had a friend who always seemed to make good grades. He wasn't a nerdy guy who studied during lunch or skipped game nights to do homework. In fact, if you were to ask me back then, I would have thought I was smarter than he was (even if I overestimated my own intelligence!). One day I asked him how he always got one of the highest grades in the class, and this is what he said: "My mom always told me that if anyone in the class could make an A, I should be that one. So, when I go into a class or take a test, I start with the attitude that if anyone can make a good grade, I will be that person."

You've probably heard that only about 1 in 10 individuals, or 10 percent, with addiction issues achieve long-term sobriety.[1] This figure can seem very discouraging—like recovery is barely possible. But there's always reason to hope, no matter the stats. I would encourage you by saying: if anyone can make it, then *you can be the one.*

In this chapter, I want to share how you, as a couple, can use that 10 percent metric to empower your relationship and overcome addiction together. When you face the facts head-on with conviction, you will unlock strength in your shared potential to triumph over addiction.

Why Is the Success Rate Just 10%?

That 10 percent represents people who are able to maintain sobriety for a year or longer by totally transforming themselves. Just 1 in 10 addicted people walk this intense road to freedom. Here are some of the reasons why success is so uncommon:

- Addiction relapses easily, making change really tough. Recovery means complete lifestyle shifts and vigilance against ongoing threats to sobriety.

- Many people avoid the huge personal changes that recovery demands. They cling to denial and old habits because they think the cost of change is too high or too uncomfortable.
- Strong physiological and psychological drives fuel addiction. Those drives resist our self-control.
- Addictions become unhealthy coping mechanisms that protect people from pain. Replacing them is scary.
- Enabling environments stop many people from making needed life changes. As I've shared, our friends, habits, and environments exert a great deal of influence on us.

I'm going to be brutally honest with you: Only by dedicating every area of life to recovery can people break addiction's grip long-term. Halfway measures lead to backslides. The 10 percent who succeed are willing to go "all in."

Building a Recovery Lifestyle

Building a recovery lifestyle as a couple has big implications for your relationship. It means that for sobriety to stick, both of you must fully commit to a holistic recovery lifestyle—not just to individual sobriety but also to total transformation of your lives together.

Key parts of your recovery lifestyle should include the following:

- Removing tempting substances from your space and guarding against behaviors that facilitate addiction.
- Skipping triggers, like parties, where others use substances and avoiding risky friend groups.
- Attending support groups and counseling; engaging sober mentors.
- Picking up new hobbies, passions, and activities to fill time.
- Creating healthy routines around sleeping, eating, and self-care.
- Trying prayer and meditation to give you focus and a sense of calm.
- Working closely with sponsors who understand your struggle.
- Practicing radical honesty with your spouse and others; letting shame go.

Without these foundational changes, relapse usually happens eventually. As I said, halfway measures lead to disappointment, while total life change builds confidence.

Reframing the 10% as Inspiration

At first, knowing the low success rate of 10 percent could stir up anxiety or make you feel like giving up. But it can also challenge you as a couple to beat those odds hand-in-hand. Decide today that you will defy expectations and prove real transformation is possible.

Let the 10 percent success rate ignite greater conviction, commitment, and purpose in you. If 1 in 10 can conquer addiction through total lifestyle change, then your relationship can too. But you must fully embrace the challenge and fight for it together.

Approach recovery as a package deal with both of you reshaping your attitudes and lifestyles. The more thoroughly you uproot addiction, the more your bond will start to flourish. Use that 10 percent figure as inspiration to make the sacrifices freedom requires.

Lessons from the 10% Who Made It

What lessons can we learn from the 10 percent who have succeeded in maintaining long-haul sobriety by completely rebuilding their lives? Their journeys offer guideposts for us to follow. Common themes include:

- Hitting rock bottom before finally surrendering and getting help.
- Surrounding themselves with other sober, focused people.
- Becoming rigorously honest with themselves and those who support them.
- Replacing addictions with uplifting passions and practices.
- Letting resentments go and focusing on their own healing.
- Making recovery central to their identities and choices.
- Drawing strength from their support communities.

The 10 percent who succeed embody vigilance, self-awareness, and hope. They show that with total commitment and a supportive community, change is possible against the odds. Let their stories motivate you to do whatever it takes.

Recovery as Restoration

Dedicated recovery efforts lead to restoration—being freed from destructive bonds so that your best self can emerge. Since addiction narrows your focus, breaking its control helps restore wisdom and wholeness to your perspectives.

There is always a way forward for those who are committed to change. If you devote your-selves completely to walking a healthier path, you will find the tools you need—wisdom, support, and perseverance. Keep recovery efforts centered on truly knowing yourself and deepening intimacy with your spouse. Hope together for the perseverance that comes from within. Let your journey show the incredible resilience of your relationship with each other.

When you reflect on that 10 percent figure, don't be filled with fear but awe—awe that despite the odds, you will find your way to restoration. Let your relationship shine as a testament to growth through adversity.

The Joy of 100% Transformation

Hold onto this truth: Your potential is far greater than the 10 percent recovery rate. You are capable of 100 percent change—total metamorphosis of your hearts, minds, and lives together.

I know recovery has many intense moments, but I also believe as you walk this road together, you will find profound blessings—freedom from these chains, closeness with each other, joy in the present, and meaningful days ahead. Your journey will offer hope to other couples still held captive to the power of addiction.

Personal Reflection

Answer the following questions:

1. What areas of my life feel out of control due to my or my spouse's addiction? How could a total lifestyle change help restore my sense of stability?

   _____

   _____

   _____

2. Do I believe deep personal transformation is possible for me or my spouse? Why or why not?

   _____

   _____

   _____

3. What feelings come up when I reflect on the 10 percent recovery success statistic? Fear? Hope? Determination?

_____

_____

_____

4. What passions or practices could we adopt to fill the void left if I or my spouse let go of addiction?

_____

_____

_____

5. Do we currently have enough rigorous honesty and accountability in the recovery journey? If not, what needs to change?

_____

_____

_____

6. Have I (the addicted spouse) truly surrendered control and hit rock bottom yet, or do I still cling to my own wisdom?

_____

_____

_____

7. What lessons can I learn from the minority who achieve long-term sobriety? How could I emulate their vigilance and commitment?

_____

_____

_____

8. Realistically, what do I need in order to persevere in my or my spouse's recovery for the long haul?

_____

_____

_____

Couple's Discussion Questions

Discuss the following with your spouse:

1. As a couple, how can we best support each other in fully committing to a recovery lifestyle?
2. What enabling behaviors do we need to guard against in our relationship that could sabotage recovery?
3. As a team, how should we constructively handle triggers, cravings, and the potential for relapse?
4. What does rigorous, open accountability look like for us? What do we need more of?
5. Have we built enough connection with supportive communities and sponsors? If not, what next steps should we take?
6. Realistically, what changes do we need to make for recovery efforts to become central to our identity as a couple?
7. How could we learn from success stories to further motivate our own transformation?
8. Are we both genuinely committed to doing whatever it takes for our relationship to thrive? If not, what inner work or conversations are still needed?

NOTES

6

COUNTING THE Ws

Marking Recovery Milestones

When a spouse is recovering from addiction, it impacts your whole relationship as a couple. The healing journey isn't just personal—it belongs to both of you. Each step forward is a win for you both, and every win matters. Marking those major and minor milestones keeps you motivated and focused on the progress you're making together, step by step, day by day. Checking goals off will lift your spirits just when you need it most.

Tracking achievements as a team allows both of you to see the full scope of the ride you're on together. There's no sugar coating it: recovery is *rough*. The lows can feel never-ending. Recording wins lets you reflect on how far you've traveled already. Progress fuels perseverance.

Why Counting the Wins Helps

In the daily slog of support groups, counseling, fighting cravings, managing symptoms, and working on relationships, it's easy for someone in recovery to get tunnel vision. You can lose sight of every mountain you've already climbed. Recovery can seem like an endless uphill battle. It's exhausting!

Stopping to acknowledge and celebrate each accomplishment will give the two of you the energy and resilience you need to keep pushing. Here's why milestones are so important:

- **They mark your wins along the road to recovery.** The journey is long and incredibly tiresome, but you'll recognize that you've already conquered tough terrain.
- **They allow you to honor each other's grit and growth.** Healing and rebuilding your relationship takes incredible strength. Milestones let you celebrate that strength.

- **They keep your eyes on the horizon so you can see health and wholeness ahead.** Even in the foggiest days of recovery and relapse, remembering the progress you've already made can brighten the path forward.

Why the Sober Clock Matters

Whether it's one day, one year, or one decade of sobriety, keeping track of time serves some clutch purposes:

- **It's proof you're leveling up on the journey bit by bit.** Recovery is about progress through tiny wins that eventually transform your life and marriage. Putting numbers on it makes the abstract real.
- **It keeps you accountable and honest, making it tougher to hide setbacks from your spouse.** You build trust by sharing the full truth.
- **Hitting milestones motivates you to keep grinding.** That is because you can see your efforts paying off and making an impact.
- **Comparing life in early sobriety versus one year in highlights personal growth.** Your whole perspective shifts as you see the entire timeline.
- **For both of you, it anchors your relationship to the present recovery journey.** Focus on the present instead of past pain stuck on repeat.
- **It creates meaningful rituals to reflect on with gratitude, cementing resilience.** You've made it this far, and you can keep on making it.
- **Every milestone reached restores hope that more sobriety lies ahead.** It reminds you that long-term freedom is possible.

Tracking time gives you a map of the recovery road you've traveled together. It also spotlights where you still need to go. But most importantly, it's the proof that you're putting in the work every day.

Leveling Up Together

I know people who are avid gamers. Some of them have played the same game for years. They get a lot of satisfaction from the accomplishments they have made, and I respect the perseverance they have. In epic video game quests, loyal teammates celebrate hard-won victories side by side. They relish leagues beaten, foes conquered, and comrades supported. Hitting milestones feels pretty fulfilling.

Addiction recovery isn't a video game, but you can envision it as the ultimate co-op adventure, especially when you are tackling it as a married couple. Early on, your squad cheers every hour and day as you resist the magnetic pull of old habits. Abstinence is a strength gained over time. Progress fuels perseverance, and you level up together as a couple.

In recovery communities, you'll notice hype around sobriety landmark celebrations. Support groups like AA or NA track progress by handing out chips memorializing hours, days, and years since someone last used. Early on, counting small wins helps establish a rhythm when you feel shaky. It's like leveling up as you transform vulnerability into strength.

Like some role-playing video games, recovery has no real "end." Marking milestones matters most when it represents revived intimacy, honesty, and hope.

You may choose to create celebrations that coincide with your recovery program, or you can create some of your own. What are some of the wins you can commemorate jointly as a married couple?

1. **Consecutive Time**—Mark another month of attending meetings and therapy.
2. **Danger Zones Avoided**—Note victories you've gained from evading toxic people, places, and triggers that once sabotaged you.
3. **Relationship Gains**—Celebrate communication improvements and steps made toward restoring trust.
4. **Responsibilities Restored**—Reclaim family game nights, meaningful vacations, and the reestablishment of duties that once were ignored.
5. **Special Days Rediscovered**—Redeem missed celebrations that you can now enjoy sober.

Little by little, recognized wins replace shame with encouragement.

Qualitative and quantitative gains show you that you are on the path toward freedom. With compassion and grit, help each other tally every level of progress. Display photographs memorializing breakthroughs. Save mementos of places you visit together, only now sober. These commemorative pictures and objects will remind you of just how far you've come.

Leveling Up Rituals

As you recognize wins, find ways to make them even more special. In any skill-building grind, consistently hitting higher levels deserves hype—so, make a big deal out of it! Recovery wins prove your resilience despite the relentless villain of addiction. Meaningful celebrations spark motivation and build hope. How can you make these moments extra special?

Creativity makes it personal. Choose a landmark goal and then brainstorm ideas together. Choose something unique to the two of you to commemorate reaching that battle victory. Here are some examples:

- **The Memoir**—Reflect on milestone wins in a journal, capturing in writing the lessons that caused you to grow. Connect your story of recovery to your ongoing, epic story as a couple. You are writing an amazing love story with accounts of win after win.
- **The Feast**—Cook a special dinner together. Offer words of affirmation and gratitude to each other. Give thanks to God for the way He has provided for you even during some very dark days.
- **The Ceremony**—Develop some symbolic rituals to remind you of why you are fighting for victory in the first place. Take these moments to reaffirm that you won't give up on each other or your marriage when things get difficult.

Consider exchanging meaningful gifts, handwritten letters, and photo albums memorializing your journey together. Get creative. What you choose to do matters less than the meaning you put into it. This is your one-of-a-kind love story, so the two of you get to choose how it is written.

By purposefully celebrating your wins, not just tallying dates and chips, you are creating the building blocks to restore your intimacy and your marriage. Allow these moments to revive the dreams you once shared on your wedding day. Here's to the victories that await you!

Unlocking New Levels

In marathon journeys like recovery, yearly sobriety milestones deserve special-edition celebrations. Whenever you have wandered in the valley of the shadow of death, another lap around the sun is a good time to tell addiction it can't have you or your marriage. You didn't die (thank God) and neither did your relationship with each other!

What creative ideas can you come up with for an annual relationship recommitment ritual? Here are some examples to get you started:

- **Set fire to the past.** Make a list of old addictive behaviors and marital hurts. Then light that list on fire. Yes, you'll want to do this ceremony in a safe manner, but find a way to completely dispose of those "old" things. Then commit to a new path for your marriage and for future generations.
- **Take a relaunch trip.** Return to the place you first committed to recovery from addiction. Remind each other of the radical change you embarked on that day. Savor

the moment. You may not be where you want to be yet, but you've come a long way since that day.

- **Re-declare your covenant.** Renew your marriage vows or write fresh, new ones. Reinforce your dedication to each other. Take this moment to release old shame and embrace a renewed love.
- **Start a new anniversary tradition.** Choose something special to celebrate and reconsecrate your relationship. As you think about the victories you have won, dream about the adventures that lie ahead.

Then feast well because, by grace, you have made it this far. In fact, you're just getting started. Pour your favorite (non-alcoholic) beverage and raise a glass to each other and the future!

Avoiding the Speed Bumps

Reveling in the wins is great, but you also need to keep your journey in perspective. Sometimes you'll encounter unexpected hazards. How do you avoid potholes while still celebrating progress?

- **Curb any cockiness.** Don't let major gains sabotage your vigilance against old enemies who are plotting comebacks. Stay shrewd yet humble. Don't leave any margin for error.
- **There's no shame in stumbles.** When minor falls or failures happen as they sometimes do after achieving new heights, learn to bounce back more quickly. Setbacks are built into any epic quest, so give yourself some grace.
- **Quality is greater than quantity.** Big numbers in recovery might impress your friends, but courageous daily choices have even more power. Do small things right every day.
- **Feelings matter too.** Beyond tracking numerical stats, acknowledge emotional, spiritual, and relational strides as good ways to measure recovery.
- **Stay flexible.** Don't chain yourself to arbitrary dates or let unrealistic expectations set you up for disappointment. Grace offers some wiggle room.

This adventure's filled with twists and turns that no guidebook can ever fully cover. Learn which milestones matter most to you and your spouse and celebrate them. This is your journey together.

The Ultimate Achievement

Beyond bragging rights, leveling up in recovery together unlocks the gift of deep intimacy over time. It exposes who you genuinely are, what really matters, and the full scope of your potential as you tackle new challenges together. Your bonds will grow stronger as you take on new enemies as one unified team.

If you keep a journal or a diary, you will be amazed at the insights you have gained as you glance at the past. There are still more adventures awaiting you. Counting wins marks your journey together; they are not the endpoint.

So, keep climbing and keep counting. Let your time in recovery become a living history of overcoming against the odds. Keep grinding! *The real reward is the growth.* You are destined to win!

Personal Reflection

Answer the following questions:

1. What are some recent wins in the recovery journey that I can celebrate?

   _____

   _____

   _____

2. What are some upcoming milestones or goals my spouse or I can achieve?

   _____

   _____

   _____

3. What are some ways we can creatively commemorate sobriety milestones?

   _____

   _____

   _____

4. How has tracking recovery time helped restore accountability and motivation in our relationship?

_____

_____

_____

5. What are some past hurts in our relationship I need to let go of as I move forward?

_____

_____

_____

6. What are some areas of emotional and spiritual growth I've experienced through the recovery process?

_____

_____

_____

7. How do I typically respond to minor setbacks in recovery? What can I do to improve in this area?

_____

_____

_____

8. How has the recovery journey deepened my intimacy with my spouse?

_____

_____

_____

Couple's Discussion Questions

Discuss the following with your spouse:

1. How can we create meaningful rituals to celebrate sobriety milestones together?
2. What are some creative ideas we could try for an annual recommitment ceremony?
3. How has recovery deepened our intimacy and strengthened our marriage?
4. What challenges related to the recovery journey do we still need to overcome as a couple?
5. How can we best support each other through minor setbacks if they happen?
6. What hopes and dreams for our future are being restored through this process?
7. What anniversary tradition could we start to celebrate how far we've come?
8. How can we make space to regularly celebrate each other's grit, growth, and wins?
9. How can we leverage our story to give hope to other couples facing similar journeys?

NOTES

7

I'M SORRY

Learning to Apologize Regularly and Effectively

We all mess up sometimes and hurt the people closest to us, even if we don't mean to. When it comes to romantic relationships, conflict is inevitable, but addiction wreaks its own unique sort of havoc on even the strongest relationships. Lying, causing hurt, breaking trust—it all leaves your spouse feeling lonely and uncared for. Healing is dead in the water if you can't talk openly and take ownership. So, when you've messed up, a sincere apology is mandatory.

But *how* you apologize after fights or disagreements makes a huge difference in whether your spouse believes you're genuinely sorry. You must show that you're tuned in to how your actions impacted your partner, that you feel their pain, and that you still value your bond. A genuine apology cracks open the door for them to potentially forgive you and start rebuilding intimacy with you. Apologizing takes guts and humility, but it's so necessary. It signals you're willing to take responsibility for the harm caused and are committed to making it right.

Please understand that words alone may not be enough to fix everything. But you have to start somewhere, and a heartfelt apology is still a huge piece of recovering from addiction's damage and redeeming the relationship. Serious vulnerability helps patch up broken trust and restores closeness when addiction has ravaged a marriage.

How to Offer an Effective Apology

If you're trying to salvage a relationship smacked down by addiction, the journey starts by learning how to apologize effectively. There's an art to crafting an apology that repairs trust and brings you closer instead of pushing your partner away. Gary Chapman and

Jennifer Thomas, authors of *The 5 Apology Languages*, break it down into the five key elements every good apology needs.[1] Let's walk through them:

1. **Show you feel their pain.**
   First, tap into some empathy and validate whatever emotions your partner is feeling—anger, sadness, betrayal, etc. Phrases like "I hate that I hurt you" and "I regret my actions" demonstrate you really care about their feelings. This helps open the door for forgiveness.

2. **Own your mistake.**
   Take full accountability without excuses or finger-pointing. Tell your spouse clearly, "I messed up. I was wrong." Don't blame them or the circumstances. Stand up and claim your mistake so your partner knows you recognize how your behavior impacted them.

3. **Make it right.**
   Sometimes words aren't enough to fix the situation. Figure out action steps to help repair things. This may include counseling, changing bad habits that hurt your spouse, or finding other ways to restore trust. Back up your words with effort.

4. **Promise you'll grow.**
   Assure your spouse that you fully intend to learn and grow from this experience. Explain how you plan to avoid repeating the behavior that damaged your relationship. This shows you're committed to personal growth as an individual and a partner.

5. **Ask for forgiveness.**
   Humbly ask your spouse to forgive you. Say something like, "I'm really trying here. Will you please forgive me?" Don't try to force an answer, though. Healing takes time. Rinse and repeat these steps as often as necessary.

There you have it: the blueprint for crafting an apology that rebuilds connection. We all mess up, but the couples who last are the ones who handle conflict in healthy ways, paving the way for trust and intimacy.

Why Apologies Matter

Maybe you grew up in a family that didn't apologize, or if they did, they didn't do it very well. It's time to disrupt that pattern and create a new way of relating to your spouse. Why do apologies matter so much? Here are some important reasons:

- Coming clean shatters secrecy and frees your conscience. Exposing destructive stuff to light helps heal what's festering in darkness.
- Apologies build self-awareness, challenging your ego's excuses. Owning your faults makes you mature and strengthens your recovery.
- The relief you'll feel after apologizing rekindles motivation and hope that your relationship can still change for the better.
- Apologizing gives your partner closure instead of brushing off how they feel. Validating their perspective lifts heavy weights off their heart.
- Taking accountability fortifies your defenses against sliding back into old, addictive patterns. Making amends builds your integrity muscle.
- Your bond shifts from being stuck in bitterness about the past to moving positively toward the future. Your energy redirects to rebuilding your relationship.

You can break many vicious cycles and improve the emotional and spiritual health of your marriage if you make apologies as natural as breathing.

Smashing Roadblocks to Apologies

For addicts used to avoiding personal responsibility, admitting where you went wrong takes battling some mental roadblocks such as:

1. **Downplaying the damage.** Counselors can help you uncover all the emotional wreckage you've ignored to avoid guilt in the past. Make a list recognizing every wound your actions have caused.
2. **Blaming external stuff.** While past traumas or mental health battles might partially explain addiction's pull, the focus should be on taking ownership of decisions you made, not deflecting responsibility.
3. **Fearing your spouse won't forgive.** Look at making amends as a gift to clear your conscience, not merely something hinging on your partner's forgiveness. Let go of expecting anything in return.
4. **Struggling to be vulnerable.** Writing letters, talking about memories with a counselor, and praying for boldness helps build your capacity to push through discomfort and get honest and real.
5. **Repeating old cycles.** Part of recovery means frequently reassessing backslides that require new apologies and course corrections. Stay committed to total transparency.

The blessing of admitting failure is realizing we're all unfinished works. We don't have to get stuck denying past wrongs, nor do we need to constantly dwell on them. We must move forward with accountability while embracing grace and forgiveness.

Why Forgiveness Is Necessary

Addiction is destructive, and everyone in its path knows it. Once a spouse finally confesses all the harm they caused, it's up to the supporting spouse to decide whether to grant forgiveness or not. Choosing to confront the pain instead of pushing it back lays an important foundation for rebuilding your wrecked relationship.

Why does forgiveness offer freedom even if the words "I'm sorry" are never spoken?

- It keeps you out of victim mode by refusing to let someone else's actions define your identity.
- It banishes the self-punishment of clinging to resentment that poisons your peace.
- It reminds you that we all mess up—even good people make horrible choices during difficult times.
- It believes people have potential beyond their worst moments to still transform.
- It pours energy into building healthy new patterns instead of stewing over past toxicity.

Forgiveness brings you peace and sets you free. Ironically, it can also nudge your spouse toward regretting wrongs when they experience mercy they don't "deserve" yet. Grace is powerful.

Now, forgiveness doesn't mean you become their enabler or act like the harm never happened. Protect your heart still. Forgive your spouse's flaws, but don't encourage ongoing bad behavior. While letting go of bitterness, don't stop demanding accountability.

Over time with God's help, responding to betrayal with compassion becomes more natural than revenge. You offer up your pain, believing your relationship can still make a comeback. Seeing your spouse's humanity underneath addiction rekindles faded passion and presents fresh opportunities to reconnect. Beauty emerges from the ashes.

When forgiveness follows an apology, reconciliation happens, slowly weaving back together a marriage that addiction once shredded. Though hard times will undoubtedly happen again, your bond will hold strong, anchored in hard-won trust that has been restored through apology and forgiveness. A stronger union will emerge as brokenness meets humility and radical love.

Personal Reflection

Answer the following questions:

1. What harmful behaviors or lies have damaged trust in our relationship?

   _____

   _____

   _____

2. What excuses do I tend to make to avoid taking full responsibility when I mess up?

   _____

   _____

   _____

3. What fears or insecurities make it difficult for me to sincerely apologize to my partner?

   _____

   _____

   _____

4. What vicious cycles do I tend to repeat that require apologies and course corrections?

   _____

   _____

   _____

5. What external factors or past traumas might explain my harmful behaviors but don't excuse my personal responsibility?

   _____

   _____

   _____

6. How can I build my capacity to be more vulnerable and honest with my partner when I fail them?

_____

_____

_____

7. What action steps can I take to help repair the damage I've caused and restore my partner's trust?

_____

_____

_____

8. How can I disrupt unhealthy relationship patterns from my upbringing and create new ways of relating?

_____

_____

_____

9. How can I pour energy into building healthy new patterns rather than dwelling on past toxicity?

_____

_____

_____

Couple's Discussion Questions

Discuss the following with your spouse:

1. What wounds from lies, betrayal, or other harmful behaviors are we still carrying that make it hard to trust and reconnect?

2. What excuses or finger-pointing do we tend to engage in rather than taking personal responsibility when conflicts happen?

3. How can we get better at validating each other's feelings and showing empathy when apologizing?

4. What vicious cycles do we tend to repeat that require ongoing apologies and course corrections?

5. How can we help each other feel safe being vulnerable about our failures, flaws, and backslides?

6. What action steps can we take together to start restoring trust and rebuilding intimacy?

7. How did our families and upbringings model good or bad ways of handling conflict and apologizing?

8. What external factors might explain our issues but don't remove our personal responsibility?

9. How can we pour energy into creating healthy new patterns rather than dwelling on past hurts?

10. How can we balance accountability with grace and forgiveness when working through betrayal and rebuilding trust?

NOTES

8

LIGHTENING THE LOAD

Letting Laughter Return

I know I'm repeating myself here, but I need to say it again: *relationships are hard!* And addiction makes them so much harder. Recovery isn't easy, or everyone would be doing it. It takes tough conversations and working through a lot of messy feelings. Rebuilding trust when so much damage is done requires some deep healing.

But don't underestimate the power of joy. Laughter connects us. A good giggle lifts our moods and reduces the tension. Share those hilarious videos that make you crack up. Learn to relax together again. Throw on a funny flick or even have your own dance party—just the two of you. Go to a comedy club. Send funny videos and emojis to each other. Find little ways to smile every day and share those smiles with your spouse.

When life hands you stress, laughter can help you cope. It reminds you of who you really are underneath all the struggles. Let that joy give you hope, lift your spirit, and reconnect you with your partner. A relationship filled with laughter can make it through almost anything.

Even solid couples who don't battle addiction go through rough patches. Recovery adds additional layers and extra challenges. Guilt, shame, anger, and hurt often swirl in marriages that are dealing with addiction. Yes, you need to talk through the messy stuff, but don't forget the power of a smile, giggle, or deep belly laugh. Laughter relieves the intensity so you can see clearly. Sprinkling lightness in your relationship helps both of you see there are better days ahead.

The Power of Laughter in a Marriage

Laughing together keeps relationships solid, and there's science to prove it. Laughing triggers the brain to release dopamine, serotonin, and endorphins—our "feel-good"

69

chemicals that boost our moods and help us relax. Cortisol and adrenaline get suppressed, which means less feelings of stress. Physically, laughter eases muscular tension, facilitates breathing, and improves blood flow. Even just anticipating times of laughter can prime us for happiness and intimacy.[1]

Shared laughter is an awesome marker of how healthy your bond is with your spouse. Researchers have found that couples who laugh during their conversations say they have more satisfying relationships. The more they share humor, the higher they report their closeness and feelings of support from their spouses. Couples who share silly private jokes and laugh together often are more likely to report relationship satisfaction and have lower chances of splitting up. Through playful banter, lovers continue strengthening their bond.[2]

Playfulness and laughter activate the body's social bonding system. Humor signals acceptance rather than judgment between partners. Walls come down, and masks slip off. With laughter's help, you communicate openly as your true selves. This builds an unbreakable sense of oneness in your relationship.

Recovery is a serious matter, but no one can be serious all the time. Go all out with giggle sessions! Share inside jokes, humorous stories, and funny videos. Make laughter a daily habit in your marriage. It just may be the secret sauce that lifts your moods and brings you even closer.

Hacking Recovery with Laughter

Humor can make the process of recovery much less tiresome in so many ways. Laughter is the ultimate recovery hack. Here are some of the things it can do for you:

- **It defuses fights.** Beefs with your spouse inevitably blow up as you navigate new boundaries. Laughter releases the pressure valve before you both snap. A well-timed laugh keeps conversations constructive.

- **It boosts resilience on bad days.** Recovery is filled with demoralizing backslides and emotional baggage dumps. Laughter lifts your spirits and encourages you to persist despite these pitfalls. It reminds you that happiness and healing can happen simultaneously.

- **It repairs broken bonds.** Addictive behaviors ruin trust and intimacy, but shared laughs create openings to reconnect. Playful vibes help you relate as partners rather than enemy combatants.

- **It adds fun to the daily slog.** Recovery feels tediously heavy 24/7. Humor forces you to chill and enjoy each other's company instead of just venting. Light moments can sustain your motivation.

- **It normalizes slipups.** A well-placed joke lets you name your fears and irritations without shame. We all mess up, and laughter makes our faults and foibles feel universal.
- **It inspires forgiveness.** Sometimes you just have to laugh at overreactions before you can make amends. Putting the drama in a humorous perspective humbles your egos and clears space for healing.

So, use humor as a tool when life gets too serious. Laughter can make the journey to sobriety way smoother.

Laugh Boosters

If you need to bring more laughter into your marriage, weave the following strategies into your daily routine:

- **Share witty conversations during chores.** Drop punchy comebacks, cheesy pick-up lines, or just learn to be goofy while you're doing mundane tasks. Finding joy in the daily grind will keep you upbeat.
- **Keep a humor log.** Record hilarious memories, inside jokes, and spicy comments in a journal. When times get tough, look back and enjoy the humor to lift your spirits.
- **Enjoy sitcoms and stand-up comedy specials.** Binge lighthearted movies and comedy shows together to get your giggle on and decompress your stress. No dark humor allowed!
- **Reenact awkward moments.** Dramatize painful recovery moments through exaggeration and funny voices. Making light of difficult experiences helps you move forward.
- **Create surprises.** Leave silly gifts and share inside jokes. Playful pranks like jump scares can be good as long as your spouse doesn't see them as mean (avoid mean). Affectionate tricks will strengthen your bond instead of creating resentment.
- **Choose cheesy nicknames.** Resurface hilarious handles from your childhood or create new nonsensical names unique to the two of you. Make sure your spouse sees the humor in it and is okay with your choice of a name (again, avoid mean).
- **Call out overreactions.** When bickering goes overboard, point out the absurdity: "We sound like cranky toddlers throwing a tantrum!" These humorous reminders will help you regain perspective.

Sprinkle these laughter lifelines into your program as a couple. Shared humor could make all the difference on thornier days.

Humor's Limits

Obviously laughter shouldn't replace hashing out real recovery challenges. Certain conversations have to get deep. Humor should never be used to mask aggression or hostility, which can hurt more than help. Jokes and laughter also shouldn't be used as a cover for failed responsibility.

However, when applied with care and wisdom, humor remains clutch for healing. Let it pierce the darkness that's been shrouding your relationship. Recovery takes grit and courage, but it's not supposed to be a joyless grind until you break. Let the healing power of humor help loosen addiction's grip.

So, sprinkle in the laughter. Find those micro-moments of levity even when life looks bleak. Stay playful, stay kind, and keep laughing together. One day you'll look back with gratitude for humor's healing power.

Personal Reflection

Answer the following questions:

1. How can I bring more laughter and lightness into our marriage? What makes me smile or laugh?

   _____

   _____

   _____

2. Do I take life too seriously sometimes? When was the last time I truly let loose and acted silly?

   _____

   _____

   _____

3. What funny memories do my spouse and I share that I can reminisce about?

   _____

   _____

   _____

4. How can humor help defuse tense situations or arguments with my spouse?

_____

_____

_____

5. Do I see the humor in awkward recovery moments and slipups? Or do I tend to spiral into shame?

_____

_____

_____

6. What are some private jokes or nicknames my spouse and I have that connect us? How has "inside humor" strengthened us as a couple?

_____

_____

_____

7. How can I surprise my spouse with a silly gift or prank to make them laugh (in a non-mean way)?

_____

_____

_____

8. Do I laugh enough every day? What gets in my way? How can I let loose more?

_____

_____

_____

9. Does humor sometimes feel inappropriate considering the seriousness of recovery? How can I learn to laugh even during difficult seasons?

_____

_____

_____

Couple's Discussion Questions

Discuss the following with your spouse:

1. What are some of our funniest shared memories from our relationship?

2. How did we use humor to connect in the early days of our relationship? How can we recreate that laughter now?

3. What sitcoms, movies, viral videos, or other types of humor make us laugh the hardest? Let's make time to enjoy them.

4. What is our love language when it comes to humor? Do we prefer physical pranks, banter, or inside jokes? Let's remember to play to each other's humor style.

5. When is humor hurtful versus helpful during conflicts we have? How can we use it as a tool and not a weapon?

6. Do we take ourselves too seriously sometimes, considering all we are trying to juggle? How can we nurture more daily laughter?

7. What funny nicknames or memories do we share privately that no one else would understand? Let's reminisce.

8. Have we lost some of our ability to just be silly with each other amidst the seriousness of recovery? How can we get that back?

NOTES

9

RESTORING INTIMACY AFTER ADDICTION

It's Not Just About Sex

Addiction shatters even the strongest bonds. At one time, you may have thought nothing could come between the two of you, but then something did—addiction. As substance use or other addictive behaviors consume one spouse, the other begins to feel them withdraw emotionally and physically. They may still want sexual intimacy, but the wounds are too deep for a satisfying physical relationship. The addicted person has shifted their attention away from meeting their spouse's needs. Deception around their behavior destroys the marriage's foundation of trust. Reckless behavior violates boundaries, creating deep emotional wounds.

At this point, you both begin to build emotional walls. The addicted spouse retreats in shame, while the wounded spouse feels betrayed and closed off emotionally. The damage starts to bleed through all levels of your connection. It spans emotional, physical, and spiritual realms.

For healing to occur, the addicted spouse must be dedicated to recovery and regaining trust. Meanwhile, the wounded partner must find space to forgive and release bitterness. Rebuilding intimacy after such deep wounds is slow, delicate work. It will require hard labor and fierce perseverance from both of you. But if both of you are committed to nurturing your relationship again, your broken connection can grow back together. It may even grow stronger. This journey toward restoring intimacy starts with both of you taking some first steps.

Laying the Groundwork

Before intimacy can bloom again, essential foundations must be reestablished. Core trust must be reinforced through consistent action over time.

As the **addicted spouse,** you must:

- Demonstrate commitment to sobriety by entering treatment, establishing recovery routines, and surrounding yourself with support communities and counselors. Do the hard internal work.
- Make amends for the harms you have caused without expecting instant forgiveness. Apologies should be followed by improved behaviors.
- Accept that regaining trust requires patient effort over years, not more empty promises. Remain dedicated to this ongoing process.

As the **wounded spouse,** you must:

- Speak up when you are hurt while also extending empathy related to the struggle with addiction. Seek education about the disease of addiction and the recovery process.
- Release resentments when possible. You don't have to condone past addictive behaviors, but you should free yourself from their hold on you. Grant forgiveness as a way to reclaim power rather than thinking of it as something your spouse is entitled to.
- Accept imperfections when your spouse makes repair efforts while also establishing boundaries. Celebrate small acts of courage and honesty without being overly critical.

As both of you nurture vulnerability and compassion, you create the right environment for intimacy to grow again.

Reconnecting Emotionally

Before you can restore physical closeness, you have to work on emotional openness in these ways:

- Share your honest feelings with your spouse so they have the opportunity to hear you and respond with empathy.
- Discuss challenging issues calmly and without criticism.
- Admit your fears, insecurities, and shame, inviting your spouse to support rather than judge you.
- Reveal your innermost struggles and wounds from your past.

Rebuilding the Relationship

Rebuilding relational intimacy requires the following:

- Check in with your partner regularly about how you both feel your relationship is going. There's a middle ground between being overly worried about every little thing versus never asking if small changes could bring you closer. Touch base to show you care about meeting one another's needs. And gently talk through any tensions before they spiral. Keeping communication open prevents disconnecting down the road.
- Work through conflicts constructively together.
- Express affection, praise, and gratitude for each other.
- Be reliable and present every day. You are rebuilding trust, so reliability is crucial at this time.

Creating New Memories

You may have a lot of negative memories in your relationship. The best way to deal with them is to replace them with new, positive ones by doing these things:

- Make opportunities for laughter, play, and new adventures.
- Tackle external challenges and hard tasks side by side. As you conquer new obstacles, you will rebuild trust in each other.

Seeking Spiritual Intimacy

Spiritual intimacy may encompass the following:

- Share spiritual practices like praying or Bible reading.
- Talk about faith with each other.
- Forgive past wrongs and give grace and mercy when either one of you messes up.
- Pray for your spouse's spiritual well-being.

Reigniting Physical Connection

By nurturing intimacy across all the areas I've mentioned, you can slowly reconnect your fractured hearts. You are starting to make your relationship feel like a safe harbor again. As your emotional bonds strengthen and you begin to repair trust, you will find that physical intimacy can reawaken in your relationship.

However, remain cautious and be sensitive, at least early on, as you restore your relationship. If you become pushy in your sexual interactions, you risk hurting your spouse even more. Wait until both of you signal that you are ready to return to physical intimacy. I don't mean for you to wait forever, but you should proceed gently. Here are some tips to help you reignite your physical passion:

- Move slowly, especially if you are the spouse who has struggled with addiction. Remember, your actions have created many wounds, so try to follow your spouse's pace for next steps.
- Frequently communicate your comfort levels before, during, and after any sexual interactions.
- Stick to sexual behaviors you both enjoy. Don't pressure your spouse into new activities until they express a mutual interest.
- Consider counseling around intimacy barriers. You may both have to work through trauma, shame, grief, or loss.
- Focus on being emotionally present. Practice gentle, nonsexual touch.
- Relearn your spouse's changing needs with patience. Things may not return to exactly the way they were before. Create a new way of interacting physically with your spouse.
- Voice sincere appreciation for any step forward your spouse makes. Recognize any progress as courageous.
- Release self-judgment when you feel like some interactions are fumbling or awkward. It may take some time for things to feel comfortable again.
- Continue nurturing nonphysical connection as the wider foundation for your marriage.

While reigniting passion requires a delicate touch, dedication yields great rewards. With time and care, physical intimacy can not only recover but can also become even better. You've fought hard for each other, and that is a victory.

How to Maintain Lasting Intimacy

As intimacy rebuilds between the two of you, create some safeguards to keep that closeness for a lifetime:

- Nurture intimacy through regular check-ins, date nights, and fun activities.
- Rigorously maintain honesty and transparency—even around uncomfortable topics.
- Recognize any emotional disconnection that comes from stress. Then work to draw each other back to closeness.

- Deal with minor hurts, conflicts, or resentments quickly before tension and pride grow.
- Express heartfelt affection through gentle touches and words of praise, thanks, and love.
- Continue making new adventures to conquer together.
- Grow spiritually as a couple.
- Laugh and share deep conversations at least as often as you have sex.
- Mark recovery milestones and relationship victories together.
- Seek help to improve your intimate communication and correct sexual problems.
- When one of you struggles with sobriety or past wounds, respond with compassion rather than anger.

You can't change the past, but each day is a new chance to write another better chapter together. Through hard work and stubborn love, you will see your fractured story transform into one of freedom and victory. Let intimacy grow again, binding up the broken places between you. The work will require patience. Don't expect perfection—because it won't be perfect. But it will be beautiful.

Special Note on Sexual Addiction and Pornography

How do you pick up the pieces after the betrayal of sexual addiction and pornography use? Rebuilding your marriage after sexual addiction is especially challenging. Your trust has been shattered. If this is your experience, I highly recommend seeking a therapist who understands sexual addiction and its effects on a marriage. They can walk you and your spouse through the messy healing process.

On top of professional support, here's some straight talk about starting to restore things:

- Learn to talk again. Being open and honest will help you slowly rebuild a safe place to share your thoughts and feelings.
- Set boundaries and live by them. Decide what healthy sexual behavior looks like for both of you to feel secure. Discuss issues like tech use, intimacy schedules, and accountability plans. Agree on the boundaries so there's no misunderstandings about them.
- Forgiveness is essential. Talk about the deep pain and hurt while also aiming to forgive. Ultimately, forgiveness is the only way you can move forward.
- Take care of yourself. Do activities that bring you joy; chill out intentionally; and lean on close friends and family. Be careful about sharing intimate details of your

relationship with all your friends and family members. Long after you have forgiven your spouse, the information you give them may cause them to keep resenting your spouse.

Healing from something as major as sexual or pornography addiction takes a ton of time and work. Be really patient and gentle with yourself and your spouse. In any case, don't go it alone. Seek help to address those issues.

Personal Reflection

Answer the following questions:

1. What positive memories or relationship strengths can I focus on amidst the pain?

   _____

   _____

   _____

2. How have my wounds and unmet needs impacted how I relate to my partner?

   _____

   _____

   _____

3. How can I balance holding my partner accountable while also extending grace?

   _____

   _____

   _____

4. In what ways have I avoided vulnerability out of fear of more hurt?

   _____

   _____

   _____

5. What emotions arise for me as we reconnect physically, and how can I communicate them?

_____

_____

_____

6. What spiritual practices could help me let go of bitterness and renew hope?

_____

_____

_____

7. How have my perceptions of intimacy changed after everything we have experienced?

_____

_____

_____

8. What are signs I still have underlying resentments that block true forgiveness?

_____

_____

_____

9. When I think about the pain caused in my marriage, where do I tend to place blame—myself, my spouse, or forces outside our control? How might I reframe this?

_____

_____

_____

10. What personal fears or insecurities might be barriers to connecting vulnerably right now?

_____

_____

_____

Couple's Discussion Questions

Discuss the following with your spouse:

1. How can we nurture trust through consistent honesty and accountability moving forward?

2. What types of professional support would help equip us through the healing journey?

3. How can we balance celebrating progress while also establishing healthy boundaries?

4. What does emotional intimacy look like for us individually right now? How can we nurture that?

5. What might help make physical intimacy feel safe and enjoyable again for both of us?

6. How will we prioritize regularly checking in on our relationship status and working through conflict?

7. What new shared activities could help us gain positive momentum?

8. What reconciliation rituals would symbolize overcoming the past for us?

9. If we notice disconnection creeping back in, what are practical ways we can reconcile?

10. How can we create space to share openly, without judgment, as we rebuild broken trust?

11. What does a healthy intimate relationship look like to us individually—emotionally and physically? How do we bridge gaps between our visions?

12. Going forward, how will we handle situations where one of us feels triggered or relapses into unhealthy patterns?

NOTES

10

BREAKING THE CHAINS OF FAMILY LEGACIES

The River That Formed Us

Long before you showed up, your family's river flowed. On the day you were born, its currents began molding you. The previous generations set so many examples, developed their own perspectives, and embraced their own beliefs. They started to instill all of those in you during your childhood. They set patterns for how you would have relationships. Some of those patterns were healthy and helpful, but some were dysfunctional and destructive. Your family's legacy river makes up a large part of your inheritance; and it played a major role in who you've become, for better or worse.

For many of us, currents of pain have churned through our families' rivers for decades or even centuries. Trauma, addiction, abandonment, and anger keep flowing downstream, threatening to drown the members of our families again and again. Mental health struggles, violence, distrust, and resentment all try to pull us under the water.

You and your spouse are the leaders in your marriage's recovery. You have been given the task of diverting the river so it won't threaten your future bloodline. It is a sober and precious calling to keep future generations away from the dangerous and lethal river and to change the course in your own marriage. It will take courage, commitment, and connection, but you can become the generational breakers. You can be the ones who stem the tide so the river no longer threatens your family.

How do you transform your family's legacy? It begins with an honest reevaluation of your family's origins while holding tight to a vision for something better. Healing will happen gradually as you take intentional small steps. This undertaking is a huge job, so don't try to navigate it alone—this is a shared journey with your spouse. Just remember that the work you put in today will change everything for those who come after you.

Examining Your Family's Origins

Start by taking an honest personal inventory of the currents that have been flowing through your family over time. Identify trends you see playing out across multiple generations. The following are some areas for you to explore:

Mental Health

Which of the following have affected your family?
- Anxiety
- Depression
- Attachment disorders
- Personality issues
- Self-destructive behaviors
- Struggles with identity
- Patterns of low resilience
- Lack of coping skills
- Other: _____

Relationship Patterns

Which of the following have affected your family?
- Emotional unavailability
- Neglect
- Verbal abuse
- Physical abuse
- Sexual abuse
- Dysfunction tied to roles or boundaries
- Codependence/enmeshment
- Other: _____

Life Skills

Which of the following have affected your family?

- Poor communication
- Poor conflict resolution
- Reckless or impulsive decision-making
- Mismanaged emotions
- Low initiative
- Lack of responsibility
- Other: _____

Addictive Patterns

Which of the following have affected your family?

- Alcohol addiction
- Substance addiction
- Sexual addiction
- Pornography addiction
- Gambling addiction
- Eating disorders
- Love addiction
- Compulsive shopping
- Compulsive gaming
- Social media addiction
- Behaviors like rage, control, or other coping vices
- Other: _____

Spiritual Approach

Which of the following have affected your family?

- Negative beliefs about God or church
- Religious hypocrisy
- Legalism
- Spiritual elitism or self-righteousness
- Absence of core values

◆ Lack of any spiritual connection

◆ Other: _____

Gaining Perspective

As you reflect on each of these checklists, you will gain some needed perspective. For example, consider these questions:

- How has the trauma, loss, or oppression that people in my family experienced in previous generations impacted my life?
- What part has biology or genetics (DNA) played in my life? Does my family have certain tendencies?
- What negative life scripts have I inherited or seen modeled in my family? Have ways of acting been embedded in me over decades?
- What societal factors have influenced my family, such as poverty or discrimination?

As you trace back the tributaries of your family's river, try to avoid piling shame and judgment on generations who went before you. They very likely fought battles you will never fully understand. Instead, learn to grow empathy for anyone in your family who has been touched by pain—whether it was 10 years or 10 generations in the past. Recognize the incredible challenges, loss, and adversity each generation faced in their own time. The aim of looking into your family's past is not to blame those who came before you but to trust that you can change the course of the river for those downstream. That is a reason to hope.

Your Shared Family Legacy

As both you and your spouse explore your families' legacies, you are beginning to create your own shared vision about the future of your family. You can commit to changing the flow of your families' rivers. Make sure to discuss the following:

- What values do we want to define our household going forward? Think about adding trust, acceptance, support, and accountability to your family's legacy.
- How do you hope future generations will describe your family's characteristics? Consider vision words such as safe, nurturing, resilient, and peaceful.
- What will be your family's spiritual legacy? Loving God and others? Service and justice? Grace and mercy?
- What relationship practices will you add to your family? Consider actions such as sharing encouraging notes, celebrating wins, apologizing quickly after

arguments, tackling challenges together, and verbalizing feelings rather than ignoring hurts.

- Distill your exchange into a one-sentence family mission statement. Let this statement anchor and guide you whenever trouble comes your way. Display it prominently to remind everyone in your home of the vision you're trying to build together.

Your legacy lives through how you choose to relate, communicate, and grow spiritually day-to-day. It's embodied through laughter over dinner, accountability for those who struggle, and rallying together as a team. As you steward your family's river today, it has power to flow for centuries.

Changing the Flow of the River

With your eyes open to the past and your vision set for the future, you now know that charting a new direction requires effort. You have to keep paddling. Progress matters more than perfection, so take small, deliberate steps. Expect some setbacks but believe you're building something better.

Carve out time to simply listen and understand each other's perspectives. After so much hurt because of addiction, being fully present for each other without distractions is crucial. Welcome hard conversations. Seek counseling when you need to work through any traumatic memories or pent-up resentments. Physical affection is important, but make sure it is wanted and welcomed.

Practice defining and enforcing healthy boundaries, especially surrounding known family wounds like addiction. Break enabling mindsets. Have awkward conversations about what behavior is or isn't acceptable in your family. Explain limits calmly and stick to them, even if other family members react negatively. Don't allow unhealthy guilt, people-pleasing, or conflict avoidance to take root in your family because those often perpetuate dysfunction.

Build a household that is stable, consistent, steady, and reliable. Follow through on promises. Establish and maintain family routines such as turning phones off at family meals or sincerely apologizing when one of you messes up. As you model dependability, you show your children what they need to thrive long-term.

Pay attention to how you each handle stress, express anger, deal with hurt, and care for yourselves. Your kids will absorb these cues on how to manage their own emotions. Verbalize feelings out loud, take a breath before reacting, and make time for healthy food and sleep. Demonstrate self-compassion when you make mistakes.

Disrupt destructive patterns by limiting or avoiding things that trigger you. These may include certain family members who are prone to drama, activities that enable or encourage addiction, or offensive content on television or the internet that fuels your rage. Surround yourselves with things that promote collective calm, laughter, adventure, and beauty.

Welcome growth and development. Learn how to build emotional intelligence as a family. Seek counseling to overcome blind spots, poor styles of communication, or attitudes of entitlement. Guide each other and your children with grace. Understand that healing is lifelong.

Make your home a peaceful and protective haven marked by joy, fun, and encouragement. Believe your family deserves to thrive, free from the weight of past generations. Stand firmly together when other extended family members resist your changes.

Renouncing Inner Vows

Alongside inherited family currents, we also accumulate baggage from our own painful experiences that threaten to sink us if not addressed. As hurts happen, we instinctually adopt self-protective mindsets or make inner vows, or promises, to shield our hearts and prevent further suffering. These inner vows may look something like these:

- "I will never let anyone have power over me again."
- "I don't need anyone—I can make it completely on my own."
- "I won't end up stuck like the rest of my family."

We adopt these secret inner vows and narratives because we think they will give us control in areas where we feel powerless. But they eventually make us uptight, unteachable, and irrational in those areas. We must identify and renounce them.

Reflect on the personal inner vows that might be hiding in the corners of your mind:

- **Finances**
  "I'll never worry about money struggles again."

- **Relationships**
  "I won't allow anyone to betray me again."

- **Parenting**
  "My kids will have total freedom. I won't try to tell them how to live like my parents did with me."

- **Family Patterns**
  "I will never be anything like my toxic parents. In fact, I will do the opposite."

- **Marriage**
  "If I can't trust them, I'm out of here."

- **Career**
  "I will be successful, and nothing will get in my way."

All of these statements are reactionary, and once we make these kinds of promises to ourselves, they become embedded in our hearts and minds. In fact, they can outlive us as we pass them on to our kids in the same way we pass on genetic traits. Acknowledging their grip on us is the first step to breaking free.

For each inner vow you have identified, do the following:

1. Renounce it openly. If you are a person of faith, place your trust in God's plan for your life rather than your own.
2. Understand that not everything is under your control, and you have set yourself up for disappointment. You can submit this area of control back to God.
3. Forgive those involved in the original hurts that triggered your inner vows. Release bitterness's hold on you.
4. Refuse to give into extremes. Bad things happen in this world, but you do not have to react to them in a way that puts you in bondage to inner vows.

We made vows because we thought we were protecting ourselves, but they were misguided. Let go of those promises that you should never have made to yourself. Your marriage can anchor the next generation to choose vulnerability, openness, and love even when life is unpredictable. That is a legacy to keep for generations.

Personal Reflection

Answer the following questions:

1. What positive legacies or strengths can I honor even when there is dysfunction in my family story?

_____

_____

_____

2. Which inherited traits or coping mechanisms could I subconsciously pass on to my kids unless I intentionally change the patterns?

_____

_____

_____

3. Which friends or mentors could support me in breaking the negative cycles I face?

_____

_____

_____

4. How has witnessing past relational patterns shaped my view of trust and vulnerability?

_____

_____

_____

5. In what ways could I be holding onto any subtle bitterness that keeps me from fully embracing our family's new legacy?

_____

_____

_____

6. In what ways have I avoided vulnerability or conflict because of past relational wounds? How could facing those wounds actually promote intimacy?

_____

_____

_____

7. Do I tend to swing to extremes as a parent because of past dysfunction I've experienced? How can I find healthy balance?

_____

_____

_____

8. When stressed or hurt, which dysfunctional coping mechanisms do I default to unintentionally?

_____

_____

_____

9. If I traced my tendencies back through generations, where would I notice similar struggles or addictions manifesting? Does that realization give me comfort or shame?

_____

_____

_____

Couple's Discussion Questions

Discuss the following with your spouse:

1. How will we handle tense conversations about family histories or blindspots wisely and gently?
2. What does healthy intimacy and support look like for our marriage right now?
3. How can we motivate each other when we feel discouraged about breaking negative patterns?
4. What family vision can we create together to steer us through future storms or setbacks?
5. How will we model and teach healthy communication and emotional skills to our kids?

6. What new shared activities or challenges could deepen our bonds as a family?

7. How can we respectfully discuss our different parenting styles and get on the same page?

8. What recovery milestones or family victories should we celebrate together?

9. How can we best support family members who still struggle with addiction or dysfunction?

NOTES

11

FAITH

A Power Greater Than Ourselves

When you're deep in the trenches of addiction, feeling crushed by bad choices and their painful consequences, it's easy to slip into denial or self-deception just to make it through the day: You rationalize the harm you're causing to yourself and others. You compromise your values with more lies and secrecy, trying to control outcomes that are uncontrollable. In isolation, any real transformation seems impossible.

Left to ourselves, we lack the internal wisdom, discipline, and strength to overcome addiction's obstacles. Addiction swallows up everything—all the physical, emotional, and environmental aspects of life. When we try to do things on our own and in our own way for too long, we often can't even envision another way out. Our best efforts and white-knuckle willpower always fail eventually. Sometimes, through much wasted time, impossible struggle, and bitter regret, we must admit we really are powerless by ourselves. Once we make that admission, we open the door to something real—something better. Once we give up trying to do things on our own, we can find hope, healing, and purpose in a power outside ourselves.

In 12-step programs, such as AA and NA, steps 1 and 2 address the concerns I have just described:

1. **We admitted we were powerless over alcohol—that our lives had become unmanageable.**
2. **Came to believe that a Power greater than ourselves could restore us to sanity.**[1]

Here's where science and spirituality converge. Evidence confirms that belief in a higher power or God provides increased social support, stress resilience, recovery motivation, a sense of meaning and purpose, and the activation of brain circuits that help override addictive impulses.[2] On psychological and biological levels, embracing a spiritual connection makes overcoming addiction more possible over the long-term.

Jesus: The Ultimate Higher Power

I want to show utmost respect for people who are not Christians or who do not believe in God at all. However, I also want to offer full disclosure: I am a Christian, and I believe that Jesus Christ will give you the best opportunity for addiction recovery. I offer that information in all humility and sincerity. I also believe Jesus provides many other benefits for those who follow Him. I have tried not to take a heavy-handed approach to faith in this book. I want your marriage to be healed and succeed. I believe doing marriage God's way gives you the best opportunity for that to happen. I also believe God will give you what you need if you honestly seek Him.

If you're feeling depleted because you've relied on your own power, I believe that God offers Himself willingly to you. He has unlimited power and can walk with you every step of the way to restore you. As a follower of Christ, I have personally put my trust in Jesus. He is humble and gentle, yet He is also the supreme Higher Power who can help you carry your burdens. When you are feeling feeble and your resources are low, He has unmatched and unlimited resources to help you. Here is what He provides:

- **Compassion**
  Another name for Jesus is *Immanuel,* which means "God with us." He was sent to be *with us* in the form of a human. He walked among people and showed deep compassion toward outcasts and people who were suffering. We can bring our heartaches to Jesus because He can relate to our pain. He's not some distant deity; He's very present and always willing to hear and help us.

- **Forgiveness**
  When Jesus died on the cross, He took the crushing weight of sin, failure, and shame. It was too heavy for us to carry, much less forgive ourselves for. In God's grace, we are released from guilt, and we stand blameless before Him. He has taken our sad, broken lives and rewritten our stories.

- **Identity and Dignity**
  Jesus gives us identity and dignity. Addiction tried to change who we were meant to be; it tried to shred our dignity and worth. Now, as children of God, we know we are

valuable, and nothing can change that. It doesn't matter how other people label us—God calls us "beloved" and "friend." We are secure and known. Jesus actually delights in us.

- **Healing and Restoration**
  Most of society condemns those who are struggling with addiction. It condemns the downtrodden. And yet, the Gospels show that Jesus miraculously healed and restored those people whom others considered "too far gone." You are never beyond God's healing and restoration in Christ. Jesus specializes in hopeless cases, reminding us that no one lies outside the reach of His redemption.

- **Belonging**
  Because of Jesus, we now belong. The Creator of the universe has taken us and adopted us as His own sons and daughters. Regardless of our relationships with our parents, God is now our Father, better than any earthly parent we could ever have. No relationship in this world can compare to the way Jesus loves us. Through Him, we have worth and purpose.

- **Freedom and Calling**
  Through addiction, we have been stuck and imprisoned, sentenced to a life of pain and self-destruction. With Jesus, our broken pasts doesn't dictate our futures. Jesus gives us freedom and a greater purpose. Our high calling is to participate in His kingdom work—we offer hope, freedom, and restoration to others who are stuck in addiction or who are victims of it.

With Jesus as our foundation, we gain the courage to walk through the hard days of recovery. His loving friendship provides shelter and direction when the rest of life feels hostile and confusing.

Relying on Our Partnership with God

Acknowledging our powerlessness opens the door, but change requires us to take action. We must surrender control to God daily. We have to trust Him for the outcomes rather than our own self-will. As we put Jesus first in our lives, He gives us His wisdom, which is greater than our own.

What does it mean to actively rely on Jesus as your Higher Power?

- **Prayer**
  Make prayer the compass that guides each day. Let it shape your decisions instead of relying only on your own emotions and wisdom. Ask God for strength to align your plans with His path.

- **Bible Study**
  Study the Bible to discover Jesus' true character. Embrace His promises instead of giving in to worry or resentment. Trust Jesus to take care of your past. Rely on Him when your circumstances feel overwhelming. Let God's Word detoxify your thinking and habits.

- **Trust**
  Outsource your anxieties to God, trusting His competence and care rather than trying to micromanage and manufacture your own solutions. Trying to act all on your own is exhausting and fruitless. Trust Him to direct and equip you.

- **Radical Honesty**
  Be honest about your role in addiction and dysfunction. Take ownership for your part in past hurts but acknowledge that Jesus supplies redemption and restoration. Let go of trying to play God in your own life.

- **Community**
  Step into community with other believers, particularly those in recovery. Together you can share your burdens without judgment and speak hope over one another. Fellow believers help us to align our lives with God's kingdom values rather than society's ever-changing standards.

- **Reliance on God's Strength**
  No matter how devastating your current struggles may be, allow Jesus to grow and deepen your faith. Stop turning to counterproductive coping methods. Let difficulty reveal where you are still relying on yourself rather than handing God control. Allow Him to enter the situation and bring complete healing rather than relying on temporary fixes.

- **Growth and Maturity**
  Move beyond a surface-level faith into complete abandonment to God's purposes. You may only see part of the picture now, but what God has planned for you is far greater than anything you can think or imagine. As you grow and mature, you will see your circumstances through supernatural, spiritual eyes rather than looking at only what your natural eyes can see.

God's calling on your life is not just about admitting your powerlessness—it is also about discovering the empowerment He gives you so you can walk in freedom and purpose. You may begin by saying, "I can't do this," but that only makes room for you to say,

"But through Christ's strength in me, I can endure all things" (see Philippians 4:13). We gain strength as we put our complete trust in Him.

Three Become One

As you invite God into your life and marriage, two cords become three, like a rope that is infinitely stronger by adding a third cord (see Ecclesiastes 4:12). God becomes that ever-present third cord who brings harmony and strength to your relationship. You can't manufacture that kind of power on your own. Christ will bind you independently and draw you toward Himself and one another simultaneously. Jesus can move between two hearts of people who have submitted themselves to Him. He then repairs, reconnects, and infuses your marriage with both human and divine love.

As Christ weaves grace into your marriage, you will find that where there were once gaps, He has filled them. He will give you love in your marriage so that when one of you falls, the other will lift them up. When both of you unravel, He will meet you with compassion to transform your tattered cords into something beautiful and strong.

There is no power or force greater than God, yet He works in us gently and intimately. We can rest in the promise that no matter how deep addiction has dug the pit, He can pull us out of it and refill the hole. Now matter how far we have wandered away, He goes to find us and bring us back home (see Luke 15:1–7). Anchored in Christ's unchanging love, our marriages can be healed and given new purpose, so when the storms come, He can help us withstand them.

When we join our marriages to God and we partner with Him, He gives us power in our weakness (see 2 Corinthians 12:9). There is nothing too broken for Him to restore. As you take Him into your marriage, you will be able to testify to His unfailing love and power to defeat any of the giants you've been facing. The battle belongs to the Lord (see 1 Samuel 17:47). Through His relentless love, He has already secured absolute victory on our behalf at the cross two thousand years ago. Nothing can defeat His unlimited love and power:

> And I am convinced that nothing can ever separate us from God's love. Neither death nor life, neither angels nor demons, neither our fears for today nor our worries about tomorrow—not even the powers of hell can separate us from God's love. No power in the sky above or in the earth below—indeed, nothing in all creation will ever be able to separate us from the love of God that is revealed in Christ Jesus our Lord (Romans 8:38–39 NLT).

And I would add—*neither can addiction separate us from God's love.*

Personal Reflection

Answer the following questions:

1. What feelings arise for me when faced with the idea of surrendering control to a Higher Power? Fear? Relief? Skepticism? Openness?

   _____

   _____

   _____

2. Do I tend to bottle up shame, or am I able to confess my personal weaknesses and struggles to God and others?

   _____

   _____

   _____

3. What spiritual practices most powerfully help renew me and connect me to God?

   _____

   _____

   _____

4. How could relying on a faith community for support lift some burdens I am currently feeling isolated under?

   _____

   _____

   _____

5. Are there any ways I still blame others to avoid looking honestly at myself and my part of addiction or dysfunction?

   _____

   _____

   _____

6. Do I spend energy trying to micromanage outcomes, or do I sincerely seek God for guidance and strength? Explain your answer.

_____

_____

_____

7. In what areas do I still struggle to fully trust God rather than hold to my own narrow understanding?

_____

_____

_____

8. How could embracing "powerlessness" over addiction actually empower me?

_____

_____

_____

9. What specific promises in the Bible ignite hope in me?

_____

_____

_____

10. Am I willing to get profoundly honest with at least one other trusted person about the places I feel most stuck? If so, what is my plan to do it?

_____

_____

_____

Couple's Discussion Questions

Discuss the following with your spouse:

1. How could we rely on other believers to walk alongside us in the recovery journey? Where might we start building that support network?
2. What spiritual practices could help us reconnect during times of tension or disconnection?
3. What guiding values do we want to shape our relationship and household going forward?
4. How can we lovingly call out unhealthy coping mechanisms in each other while still extending grace?
5. How can we speak hope and life over each other when we feel worn down in this season?
6. How can we tangibly rely on God's strength to carry burdens that feel too heavy alone?
7. How can we motivate each other when one of us feels discouraged—like transformation seems impossible or the process is too challenging?
8. If we notice the other tending toward isolation when struggling, how can we lovingly encourage seeking community or counsel while respecting autonomy?
9. How will we handle situations where one person feels spiritually apathetic while the other experiences renewed purpose and connection? How can we bridge this gap with empathy and offer helpful encouragement?

NOTES

12

GIVE THEM HOPE

Telling Stories of Recovery and Restoration

In this chapter, I will be sharing my personal story. I intentionally waited until now for two reasons: First, I don't want my journey to distract from this book's purpose: *to help restore marriages damaged by addiction.* Second, by saving my story for the end, you can see where I applied the principles I outline in this book and where I didn't. You'll also see that when I didn't, things did not go well for me.

You may wonder how I'm qualified to advise you if my first marriage failed due to my addictions. Fair critique. I fumbled through countless mistakes that I hope you can avoid. I wasted years numbing my pain instead of facing it. My ignorance, denial, and self-destruction hurt those closest to me. I own all that. I share my faults openly so you can learn from them but also so you can find hope for your own story.

Using Our Stories to Share Hope

Once stability takes root after addiction ravaged your life and marriage, you'll feel an urge to share pieces of your own journey with others. Recovery stories hold power—they remind couples who are still struggling and trapped in shame, "You're not terminally unique. Healing happens."

When you share your own vulnerability, it connects with those who are still struggling. Prisons of isolation and sinister lies start to unravel. Keeping secrets in the dark perpetuates this stigma: "No one can possibly understand the chaos we're living in." But as couples caught in the grip of addiction witness other couples march into freedom and light, they start to have hope—"We can do this."

How to Tell Your Story

Telling your story does carry risks. If you share too soon, you can reopen painful wounds that still need time to heal. And without self-awareness, it's easy to boast about your recovery with pride. When sharing your story with others, you need humility so they can receive your journey as hopeful. Communicate redemption gently. Recovery shouldn't be carried around like a personal trophy. Rather, it is a roadmap to show others the way forward.

How, then, can you shape your story to be most helpful to those who are struggling? The following are four guidelines to help you along the way:

1. Examine Your Motives

Examine your motives that exist below the surface. As you reflect on your motivation for telling your story, carefully consider which details are appropriate to share. If you need help forming what to say and how to say it, ask for wise counsel from others who have been in recovery a long time. Are you focusing on grace, hope, and compassion, or are you seeking a personal platform? Of course, it's not wrong to have a desire to grow your influence, but make sure it's in proper proportion. Don't substitute pride for hard-fought wisdom.

2. Temper Vulnerability with Discretion

There's something to be said for a little discretion. It serves no one to share every gory detail of your addiction journey. Wisdom and discernment will allow you to distinguish between what must be shared and what may be better left unsaid. Recalling all the details of your addiction journey also risks triggering yourself or your listeners who are still battling trauma and addiction. Consider your audience and appropriate boundaries judiciously. If you need help, again, ask for it from seasoned individuals and couples in recovery.

3. Identify the Real Hero

You want to comfort and guide other battle-weary couples, not make yourself the hero of your own story. If we are honest about addiction stories, there are no heroes except God. In other words, don't rewrite the story and leave the real hero out of it. The only part of the story you can genuinely own is that once you were lost but now you are found. One day, you finally surrendered yourself to God and the process of recovery. That's the best part of your story.

4. Uplift the Weary

By humbly sharing pieces of your own complex story of restoration, you lay out the pathway for other couples who are still stumbling and stranded. You remind them, "Where you are staggering today, I was once there too. Then once I surrendered my life, strength was restored and the way became clear." Your story and presence can give them the courage to take the next step.

Here are some parts of your story you may want to highlight as you tell it:

1. **Focus on the surrender required first.**
   Admit the hard truth—you couldn't save yourself or change on your own. You needed a power outside yourself to come along and help you.

2. **Humanize the struggle.**
   Avoid rose-colored hindsight. Don't make it seem like your struggle was easy. Share real moments when you wrestled despair, made painful missteps, or almost gave up.

3. **Offer breadcrumbs of hope.**
   What specific resources, people, or communities assisted you in finding breakthrough when you ran out of strength? How can these help your listeners?

4. **Remind your listeners that falling down is normal.**
   Everyone makes mistakes and then repeats them. Some of us repeat them many times. We experience temptations and setbacks. Sometimes we just want to run away. Tell them how you found grace and help in those difficult places.

5. **Assure them that their story isn't over.**
   There may be many chapters they wish they could erase, but life keeps writing. The good news is that they can change the plot. The story doesn't have to end in disaster. Help and hope are available when they are willing to surrender control and do the work.

My Story

Consider me a person with scars to show for the battles I've survived. I lost relationships and opportunities I can never get back. If it weren't for God's grace and forgiveness, I would continue carrying heavy regrets from choices I made under the influence. Had I applied the tools outlined in this book earlier on, perhaps my personal losses wouldn't have been so drastic. If I knew then what I know now about boundaries, self-care, available support, and open communication, I'm sure at least part of my story would be different. Nevertheless, God allowed me to learn from some really traumatic experiences, ones I hope you will not have to go through.

But part of how I evolved enough wisdom to write this book came precisely from screwing up epically, hitting rock bottom emotionally, undertaking the brutal self-work of recovery, and finding grace and mercy from a God who was not yet finished with me. All those hard-won lessons now allow me to be an effective resource for others. My goal here is not self-promotion. I simply want you to avoid unnecessary suffering in your life and marriage. Let my journey inspire you to believe that redemption *is* possible. We all make mistakes, but help is available to turn your life around.

You'll likely find a lot of similarities between my story and your own or your spouse's. As I tell you about my background, I will focus mostly on my addiction and how it impacted my relationships and life choices. I remember learning in treatment that when addiction first starts, your brain's maturity gets stunted at that age. My first blackout drunk episode happened around age 12 or 13. So, as you read about many of the choices I made after that, you'll understand that I often behaved like a young adolescent largely because I got stuck in my emotional development as a young teen.

Born in 1979, I grew up in South Carolina. My parents worked extremely hard. We weren't impoverished, but we did live in a small trailer. My parents had some marital struggles at times, like separations and conflicts, but ultimately they worked hard to stay together, make amends when needed, and break negative family cycles. I honor them for all they did for our family. My dad worked very hard, as did my mom.

Even so, by high school, I knew I wanted more out of life than what I'd seen so far in my home community. I lived in a tiny rural town with just a few hundred residents. My graduating class had 68 people. I wanted to surround myself with older kids and experience what they were experiencing. I tried to gain a reputation as someone who fit in with everybody. I first tried marijuana and had my initial blackout drunk episode in middle school. Looking back, I realize I did those things to impress the older kids. Like many teens, I started smoking cigarettes and pushing boundaries to seem cool and feel accepted.

But my biggest motivation at the time was knowing I didn't want to remain in that small town forever. After graduation, I got a job an hour away in Augusta, Georgia, but still commuted from my small hometown. I had a fake ID so I could buy my own beer, and I started drinking most days on my drive home after work. It's amazing what you can rationalize when you really want to drink or take drugs.

By the time I reached my early 20s, I was still hanging out with older crowds. Over the next decade, I did a lot of blackout drinking and became a full-fledged alcoholic and addict. I didn't discriminate—I was hooked on alcohol, cocaine, crack, pills, and more.

I remember dating several women and trying to "find myself" in my early adulthood. I didn't want to get married or have kids at a young age—I just wanted to experience life "my way." Those selfish motivations led me to drinking and using at work, getting fired for failing random drug tests, and bouncing between jobs. Still I kept doing things my own dysfunctional way.

I knew I had a problem but wasn't ready to face it.

After the tragic terrorist attack of September 11, 2001, the Transportation Security Administration (TSA) was hiring. I needed a job, I lied on my application, claiming I'd never been fired before. They hired me without discovering the truth—yet. I had never flown on a plane before, but at 23 years old I got to ride on airplanes as I worked across various states. For a time, I was sent to Ketchikan, Alaska. That was a long way from my small South Carolina hometown. However, I was blackout drinking, sometimes even while on the job. Working with the TSA allowed me to travel all over the United States, but I brought my alcoholism and other addictions along to every new place.

In the middle of all that addictive behavior, I was intimate with any woman who would give me the time of day. Looking back, my first sexual experience was somewhere between age seven and nine with an older girl who was supposed to be babysitting me. That experience messed with my head a lot more than I realized for a long time. Combined soon after with alcohol in middle school, I didn't learn to give proper respect to women or relationships. I was also exposed to porn during that time. I lost my virginity shortly before middle school in a traumatic way. I didn't understand it as trauma at the time, but that early event along with no proper teaching about sex impacted how I viewed intimacy and treated partners long into my adulthood.

Alcoholism made me delusional in many ways. While blackout drinking in Ketchikan, I even thought that switching liquor types would prevent blackouts. That's the first time I looked up a phone number for Alcoholics Anonymous (AA). I had a question: would changing from Canadian Club or Crown Royal to vodka fix things? I ignorantly thought the color of the liquor I was drinking would prevent me from blacking out! I wasn't interested in attending an AA meeting; I was still looking for a loophole out of my addiction.

I knew deep down I needed to get my life together, though. I thought maybe settling down with the right woman and getting married could help me grow up and change. However, it wasn't long before some of my lies caught up with me. The TSA discovered I had falsified my initial job application by saying I had never been fired from a job (when actually I had been fired from two).

So, I ended up back in Augusta, Georgia, working at the very jail where I would later be held for my first and second DUI offenses. I kept thinking major life changes would fix my issues, all while avoiding the real problem—addiction was controlling my life and destroying my relationships.

After returning to Augusta, I reconnected online with a woman I hadn't seen in years, who had previously dated my old roommate. I met up with her, had dinner, fell into a relationship quickly, and less than a year later, I proposed. I loved her deeply. We had two beautiful kids. However, we bonded over our similar destructive lifestyles. Our relationship revolved around using together, even though we still held jobs. At one point, I was a career firefighter/EMT, while she worked in insurance.

We were married about nine years, but I wasn't a good husband. We tried hard to make it work, but our connection was built on our after-work and weekend drinking and occasional cocaine use. We were escaping reality together by partying, while still trying to function as parents and bill-payers. The lifestyle that drew us together tore us apart over time. Even so, I loved being a dad. That role helped me see there was more outside of myself to live for. But my using didn't stop. I blackout drank and nearly killed my kid once when I rolled my truck.

My drinking was affecting my thinking. I'd count down the minutes during my 24-hour firefighter shifts until I could day-drink and use cocaine at home after. Meanwhile, I was watching over our baby son who was still in diapers while my wife worked her shift. I'd tone down my drinking an hour or so before she got home so it would appear I was just a little buzzed but not drunk.

Toward the end of our marriage, I checked into a mental health facility in Aiken, South Carolina, and admitted to my wife that I had an alcohol addiction and couldn't quit. After getting out of that short rehab stint, she gave me an ultimatum—if I fully committed to recovery, we likely wouldn't stay together. She didn't want to stop using, but I knew I had to, and that ultimatum terrified me. I wanted to remain married and see my kids every day. I didn't want to fake-function in an unhealthy relationship forever, but I didn't want to lose my family either.

I knew I desperately needed help with my addiction, but I felt torn trying to decide what to prioritize—getting sober or keeping my family intact. It seemed like an impossible choice without a good solution. I wanted both recovery and my wife and kids in my life, but they seemed mutually exclusive.

So, I chose to return home and work on things with my wife, but we never addressed the root problems in a way that truly made life better for her or our kids long-term. We had a few trial separations, but the last split happened after my second DUI, which occurred on our anniversary night. We had gone out to celebrate and then gotten into an argument, and I left her behind at home. Later that night, incredibly drunk, I passed out in the drive-through line of a Taco Bell. The police showed up, and that was the final blow to my marriage. My drinking had escalated to putting myself and others in danger, regardless of how much my wife cared for me.

Soon after I got out of jail, my wife and I entered into a separation. I moved into a shelter that was mainly for women, but the man who owned it had built some smaller units for men behind the main building. I was allowed to stay as long as I didn't drink or attempt to talk to any of the female residents. I kept my job and could still see my kids on the weekends, but I was miserable. When I got caught drinking in violation of the rules, the owner kicked me out for non-compliance.

I felt like I had no options—no spouse, no place to live, and a strained relationship with my kids. Though I'd been homeless and slept under bridges before, this time it felt different. I still had a family who was dependent on me, but I was in danger of losing connection with them.

I felt so hopeless that I wrote a suicide note saying I was going to end my life. My wife had left me; I couldn't envision how I would be able to see my kids again; and I couldn't find purpose or meaning to keep going. In my despair, I attempted suicide. Later, I regained consciousness in the emergency room, saved despite my intentions. My parents were there and signed legal custody forms to care for me as their adult son in crisis. At 29 years old, I moved back in with them, back to the small hometown I had so desperately wanted to leave behind.

Despite not being formally divorced yet, my wife and I were fully separated at that point. I originally left my hometown around age 18, and after nearly 10 years on my own, adjusting back to small town life with my parents was incredibly difficult. I felt like a failure for having my life unravel to the point of needing to depend on them again as a 29-year-old. I didn't want to rely on anyone to survive. But with my wife gone, I didn't have a choice other than starting the uphill climb again from rock bottom.

Even after facing real consequences, I was still drinking and using drugs. Between expensive car insurance, child support, and low-paying work in my hometown, I could barely afford rent for the small trailer I moved into after leaving my parents' house.

Living there alone, I got hooked on crack, borrowing or stealing what I could to fund my habit as life unraveled. I stole prescription pills from my sick landlord. I even gave my dealer my kids' toys and some appliances to pawn for drug money. I remember trading household necessities just to get what I desperately chased.

There was another time I tried to end my life. It was while I was staying in that little trailer. One of the town residents had asked if I was an alcoholic because I was drinking every day. They could actually smell the alcohol on me. When you first start drinking, you might wonder if people notice it on your breath (they probably do). But when it becomes a daily habit, the harsh truth is your whole body gives off the smell since it seeps out through your pores. The thought of someone uncovering my secret led me down the path of self-harm again. If I had been thinking clearly, I would've realized the truth—my drinking was never actually hidden at all, and most people already knew.

One morning, about a week later, I surveyed the tiny living room of that rental trailer. I noticed there was only a bed, a TV, a military cot for a couch, and no other furniture left. I also had no running water due to unpaid bills. I was surrounded by empty liquor bottles. My addiction had led me to a place of true destitution, devoid of any normal comforts and disconnected from loved ones I'd betrayed, but I still couldn't stop using.

So, that same morning, I went to my dealer and asked him to front me $60 worth of crack without money upfront, promising to pay later. I also had a pint of Canadian Club. Then I drove to a cemetery to smoke crack and drink. It was 7:30 am, and I should have been getting ready for work. When I finished smoking and drinking, I realized I felt nothing. I returned to the trailer and laid on the bare mattress in the living room. I was supposed to be at work by 9 am, so at 8:30, I called in sick.

But then I made a second call that morning. It was to Alcoholics Anonymous. The AA representative who answered could tell from our call that I urgently needed inpatient treatment given my severe situation. Since I worked in local government, I had state health benefits. I checked the mental health number on the back of my insurance card and was connected to a treatment center in Florida. In a moment of clarity and willingness, I did all the legwork to get admitted into the facility.

But before I could enter treatment, I spent a week in jail. Unbeknownst to me, the town mayor, my mom, and two police officers had come to my trailer to pick me up for panhandling—how embarrassing!

When I was released a week later, I called the Florida treatment center again. However, they said they consider a week in jail as a "detox." They wouldn't admit me unless I was actively using—and addict logic made me consider going out to quickly buy more drugs so I could meet their criteria. Thankfully, the person on the other end stopped me and found a way to get me into treatment anyway.

Arriving at the Florida Center for Recovery felt like pressing life's reset button. I was nurtured and cared for, feeling healthy for the first time in years. I knew a lot needed fixing, but I sensed an impending positive change even without knowing exactly what that was yet.

After my 30 days at the recovery center, fear crept in about having to leave with nowhere to go. I didn't want to go back to my parents' house, and they probably didn't want me there either. With my wife and I fully separated and that relationship fractured, I couldn't go back to her. So, I ended up in transitional sober living housing in Lexington, South Carolina.

There, I found a job working at a small restaurant I could walk to. For three or four months, I established a simple routine in supportive housing, working an entry-level job, avoiding old triggers, and building stability in recovery.

After four months sober, my wife and I cautiously decided to try reconciling. I explained to her that I couldn't go back to any substance use at all for this to work. She came to pick me up so I could move back home. Finally seeing my kids daily again was incredible. I searched hard to find a solid job, eventually landing a great one.

But our story didn't have a fairytale ending. We made it about nine months until we mutually realized that sobriety had changed me so much that, while we'd always be friends, we weren't compatible as partners anymore. And frankly, neither of us wanted to do the work truly required to reconnect on that deeper level again. I tell this story with openness because sometimes spouses can't find a way to work together toward sobriety along with restoring the relationship. I believe if you will do both simultaneously, then your relationship can be rekindled. But if either of you are not committed to both sobriety and relationship restoration, the relationship will likely disintegrate.

Though it was painful, we accepted that our marriage relationship was ending. Our priority became co-parenting our boys with grace and stability. My transformation didn't lead to what I had hoped for our marriage, but it led me to the personal growth I needed. I needed sobriety, and I needed to learn how to be the husband I was called to be.

Nine months after reuniting post-rehab, I made the difficult decision to file for divorce. There were many factors involved, but I'm going to keep those details to myself. About 30 days later, the divorce was finalized. I was awarded full custody of our two young sons, who were three and four years old at the time.

So there I was—newly sober, independent, solely responsible for two preschoolers, and with no place to go yet again. But this time, I couldn't fall back on others as a safety net. Supporting my boys depended entirely on me. We moved into a small apartment together, getting by on my paycheck plus child support, just the three of us.

Becoming a single dad to two young boys, I worked hard to maintain normalcy when everything felt uncertain. With the divorce finalizing close to Christmas, I got our tree and my sons' familiar bedsheets from my ex0wife's house so our new place would feel like home.

We initially moved into an apartment before renting a small house from a friend—an upgrade to a proper home instead of an impersonal apartment building. I got the kids a puppy and tried providing little touches of childhood magic.

Juggling the full parenting role was incredibly difficult. Children need nurturing care, a listening ear, and gentle wisdom—things I had to learn and then provide to my sons without an experienced mother figure around. But love powered me through that steep learning curve.

As a single dad, I stayed committed to my 12-step recovery meetings, attending at least one a day and collecting sobriety chips to mark milestones. For my one-year chip, the boys came with me to celebrate.

Then we got invited to attend Stevens Creek Church in Augusta. I'd tried church before, and it never clicked. But Stevens Creek was like finding the right gym, where you want to keep showing up. This time, with the only questions being why they waved hands and some other things unique to the church, we decided to give it a chance. Just like with recovery meetings, sometimes it takes finding the right fit to feel comfortable enough to be vulnerable and actually do the work.

I was skeptical about church at first. I knew some stuff about Jesus, but I lacked any real spiritual understanding. But because of that invitation, with Easter approaching, I took my sons with me one Sunday morning. It was unbelievable—like Pastor Marty was speaking directly to me. I remember crying those first several Sundays as I heard familiar terms that sounded like my recovery meetings. I was beginning to make the connections. I heard phrases like "higher power," "making amends," "quickly admitting wrongs"— important concepts that strengthened my resolve as I worked to maintain my sobriety. The spiritual principles I learned at Stevens Creek added to my progress, teaching me that I didn't have to rebuild life all by myself.

Between working the program and pursing a new faith, I started to see positive results in my life beyond simply maintaining sobriety. Having had emotional guardrails up most of my life, opening up to a community that supported my growth was incredibly impact-ful, even if unfamiliar at first. It gave me and my boys a bigger family—one that we really needed.

Attending church regularly, I started praying in gratitude for both the good and bad things that happened. Life didn't transform overnight. Even so, I volunteered to serve on the church's safety team each Sunday.

I wasn't looking for romance, but as a single dad, people wonder about you. Then this blonde-haired woman caught my eye. She seemed way out of my league. I figured she probably grew up in a nice house in the city, spoke differently from me, and certainly didn't have my accent. I made assumptions that she wouldn't relate to me or want to be with someone with kids. She might not ever want kids.

I was too intimidated to approach her, but I knew she was friends with someone I was connected to on social media. I remember scrolling through that mutual friend's Facebook account, praying that this mystery woman had a picture somewhere so I could find her profile and message her directly.

After my divorce, I had casually dated a bit but nothing serious. This time, I wanted to genuinely respect women, not see them as objects. My goal was to find someone as invested in caring for me as I was willing to invest in them. That included embracing my sons. So, I nervously reached out to Kristen online after scoping out her Facebook profile. I was attracted to her for more than her looks—I had a gut feeling she would be a positive force that would help steer my life's direction. After all the destructive paths of my past, I really wanted to grow.

At first, Kristen thought I was just some overly friendly church guy making sure she felt welcomed. But then I explained what I actually wanted to do was ask her out. I anxiously awaited her reply.

At church, I'd learned amazing things happen when you simply focus on the next right choice in front of you. Pursuing and getting to know Kristen felt like my next right step. I wanted more out of life than surviving day-to-day. I wanted to thrive. Kristen represented a partner to share that journey with—someone to build something beautiful with, brick by brick, founded on trust and vision. She was the embodiment of the new beginning I needed.

Kristen said yes to a date. I wanted to wow her, but I had to think creatively on a tight budget. In Augusta, for $100 at the time, you could charter a small plane that took you on a 30-minute sunset flight over the lake before returning to the airport for included snacks like cheese and wine. Of course, I couldn't drink wine, so I booked our adventure, requesting sparkling grape juice. It was a wonderful night.

We hit it off instantly. In my excitement, after only one date, I prematurely updated my Facebook status to "In a Relationship" with Kristen. I came on too strong, trying to stake my claim. She understandably felt overwhelmed by me broadcasting our budding connection so publicly, so we ended up taking a two-week break. It taught me to chill out and let things progress more organically. When we reconnected, I tempered the intensity and let Kristen set the pace instead of rushing. We took our time figuring out compatibility, free from social media pressures. I learned how to court her in a healthy way after so many turbulent past relationships.

In November 2013, I proposed to Kristen. This was the best decision of my life. She made our family feel whole again. My sobriety had transformed me into a new man who wanted to be the best version of himself for her and the kids. Now married for a decade, with the inevitable ups and downs of any relationship, we have an unbreakable bond. We added a beautiful baby girl to the mix. From the ashes of my former life, Kristen helped me build something beautiful. Every day with her and our children is a blessing I don't take for granted.

My life has transformed tremendously. Embracing spirituality and the 12 steps changed everything. I openly talk about my relationship with Jesus now, whereas the old me could never do that.

I changed my playground, playmates, and play habits. I know there's more purpose ahead. I now work for Steven's Creek Church as the campus facility director of operations. Eighteen-year-old me would balk at that! But it's so rewarding

More than anything, I want this book to help heal relationships. If both people commit to doing the work, the right decisions can resurrect connection. Kristen did grow up in a brick house in the city while I grew up in a trailer in the country, but those differences make us stronger. I fight for my relationship daily and want our kids to witness healthy marriage. That is what I hope for you—that you will fight for your marriage. My ex-wife married a wonderful man, and she learned to be a fantastic spouse and mom. We cooperatively parent our boys. Not every marriage can be saved. It was too late by the time I realized how I should be a good husband.

So, that's my story. I hope yours will be even better. You have an opportunity to reclaim your life and marriage—both are still worth fighting for. Make the right decisions. The principles in this book can point you in the right direction.

Personal Reflection

Answer the following questions:

1. What parts of my story or past behaviors have I not fully owned or taken responsibility for?

   _____

   _____

   _____

2. Write a version of your own recovery and relationship story. This may be the first time you have attempted to write about it. Don't try to tell it perfectly. Write it down and improve it over time.

MY STORY

Couple's Discussion Questions

Discuss the following with your spouse:

1. Share your personal stories with each other and then ask: What new things did we learn about each other as we shared our stories?
2. When did addiction first emerge in our relationship history, and why didn't we address it sooner?
3. How can we acknowledge pain from our past together yet still hope and fight for our marriage now?

NOTES

13

WALKING WITH OTHERS THROUGH THEIR MESS

Helping Couples Navigate Recovery

You may not be ready to act on the information in this chapter for a very long time. Or you may be ready today. Either way, once your marriage has overcome addiction's treacherous grip, you hold rare gems in your hands. You will have hard-won wisdom and empathy that comes from walking through the fires that almost consumed your marriage. As you regain hope and stability, you will feel called to invest in other couples who are still wandering in the wilderness.

Your own difficult journey taught you that, with hard work, patience, and love, even relationships that have been pushed to brink can gradually be restored. In reality, you have experienced a miracle; shame was replaced with acceptance and belonging, fragile trust slowly rose from the ashes through uncompromising honesty, and deep wounds were gently mended as you learned to extend empathy and compassion to each other. Your marriage now has a solid foundation. Hope took root in your hearts. You've been through some long, dark nights, but now you know light is available for those who are seeking it. Are there still some difficult days ahead? Sure, but now you have built up the resources to face them.

Once you have reached a point of stability in your own lives and in your relationship, you can begin to help other couples walk through the turmoil of addiction. In this chapter, I want to give you some things to consider as you offer help to other couples.

Remember You Are Fellow Pilgrims

Fight the temptation to place yourselves on a pedestal. You have experiences and insights to help other couples—but not from some elevated perch. Not long ago, you were exactly in the same place they are today. Your redemption stories hold plenty of beauty but also bear the scars and failures you collected along the way. Meet people where they are with humility. As you've learned, addiction follows no formula. Continue carrying the humble awareness that you possess no exclusive wisdom or self-mastery.

Show up authentically in personal conversations, small groups, or formal mentoring opportunities. Be willing to get real about your lingering doubts, flaws, and limitations. If you are a believer, you can point others God, the only one who can heal human brokenness. Share whatever strength, peace, or perspective you've found along the way. Your honesty about your own faults and falls can make space for other couples to be honest and vulnerable about their own struggles.

Listen Intently

Avoid the temptation to rely on empty clichés just to prevent your own discomfort. Pat answers may provide some momentary reassurance, but they actually offer no substantial hope that anything can change. Stay away from quick fixes or the urge to impose your own timelines. Only God can control the pace. Offer something more genuine than that. Your relatability matters a lot more than pretending you have discovered all of life's solutions.

In your own marriage, you probably have had times when it felt like you had to deal with the problem of addiction alone, carrying all this pain and anger inside you. That's heavy stuff. Try to create space for other couples to unpack all of those feelings—the regret, the trauma, and the parts no one else knows about. Tell them they don't have to stay silent or pretend to be fine when they're not. Let them know you really want to hear their whole story so you can understand where they're coming from and that you won't be shocked or make them feel ashamed for opening up. All of us have chapters we wish we could rip out.

Reassure them that you are here with them in this process to help them bear some heavy burdens so they won't feel so alone anymore. There's freedom in bringing things into the light instead of keeping them in hiding. Reaffirm that their story matters to you, and they matter too. There's no judgment here—only space to walk through this difficult time together.

Ask Thoughtful Questions

Careful questions will help unearth problems and issues. Don't be satisfied with surface details, clichés, or ineffective spiritual platitudes. Don't shy away from gentle probing about trauma, grief, and doubts. You can ask questions such as these:

- When did addiction first take hold?
- What wounds left you vulnerable or got you off track?
- What keeps you stuck?

Asking questions will help you to understand historical hurts and assumptions that are fueling unhealthy coping. Find out about available supports through questions such as these:

- Have fear or shame prevented you from allowing family to walk with you through this?
- Have you avoided counseling, church, or support groups because you are not ready to reveal some of your deeper issues?

Find out about inner thoughts, through questions such as these:

- What core beliefs feed insecurity for you?
- What thoughts have driven some of your harmful choices?

As you ask thoughtful questions, encourage couples to envision a time when their lives and their marriage will be restored. Awaken their imagination to hope for a better future.

Share Your Own Stories Authentically

As I wrote in the previous chapter, your story holds incredible power. It offers assurance that there are better days ahead. Joy and purpose can gradually be reclaimed after walking through addiction and trauma. Use your hard-won wisdom to offer real hope to other couples. But be careful not to tell some heroic self-recovery narrative. Continually point them to God's power that is able to deliver and set people free.

Share your weaknesses as you magnify God's strength in meeting you during your darkest days. Talk about how you let go of the illusion of control and opened yourself to a Higher Power that could rewrite your story.

Offer Practical Guidance

While clichés and strict rules prove unhelpful, wise guidance is valuable. Recommend addiction-focused therapy, recovery groups, and interventions that helped guide your recovery. Share what empowers your marriage and life together.

Encourage Spiritual Openness

Don't ever coerce someone or impose your beliefs. However, you can always gently invite others to learn about your experience with God and faith. Many people wrestling with addiction describe early impressions of faith that were centered around guilt and shame. Help untangle these distortions and tell them about the healing and grace available in Christ. If they express openness, you can share additional information about church, the Bible, or other spiritual resources from which you have gained strength.

Offer Community

As I said earlier, real healing seldom happens in isolation. We need community. Help others grasp the lifeline available from supportive relationships. Isolation breeds secrecy while accountability fuels growth. Introduce them to other grace-giving people who will champion recovery and the health of their marriage.

Commit to Consistency

Respond with love and grace. When they isolate or withdraw, respond with loving persistence rather than impatience. Be a steadfast friend who will be there even if they fall or their strength is depleted.

Celebrate Progress

Train your eyes to notice small, positive changes. Have they agreed to accept support, seek a counselor, or resist falling into addictive patterns? Recognize effort and honesty. As you celebrate their courageous choices, they will gain even more strength. Assure them that even if they fail that hope and victory are still available.

Help to Establish Goals

Healing happens at a different pace for everyone. Resist comparing one person's recovery journey with another's. Even so, help them establish some realistic goals, such as seeking treatment, reconciling damaged relationships, or letting go of the idea that they can recover alone. Help them develop a plan to meet and measure these goals. Remind them of progress as you see them succeed.

Assist in Preventing Relapse

Help couples in recovery establish compassionate guardrails and bridges to maintain their personal and relational health. Check in regularly. Ask them about current stressors and high-risk triggers. Give them space to express their regrets without judgment. Remind them that you are not there to add to any shame; you are present to give them hope.

Be Patiently Present

Don't overcomplicate your support. Sometimes just showing up is the most important thing you can offer. Don't feel pressured to fix every situation. Be willing to sit in silence when words fail. Persist in pursuing connection even when it would be easier to walk away.

You have glimpsed what life looks like beyond the grip of addiction. You know about the marathon facing those who are just beginning. You have also seen that healing and redemption are available. You can show others the path you have walked and give them courage that it is possible to come out on the other side of addiction with their lives and marriages intact.

While early recovery rightfully focuses on achieving sobriety and restabilizing daily life, the long game is to mend the fractures of our relationships through compassion and reconciliation. I believe Jesus meets us in our messes, showing up relentlessly to offer us strength and healing. Our part is simply not giving up on ourselves or each other.

Personal Reflection

Answer the following questions:

1. Have I fully processed my own journey? Do I need more time to heal before trying to support others? What do I still need to process?

_____

_____

_____

2. Am I humble and aware of my limitations when supporting other couples, or do I act like an expert?

_____

_____

_____

3. Am I patient with the recovery process, understanding everyone has different time-lines and paths? How could I improve?

_____

_____

_____

4. Have I surrounded myself with wise mentors who can give me feedback as I support other couples? If so, who are they?

_____

_____

_____

5. Am I genuinely concerned for the couple's overall well-being, or am I mostly trying to fix situations? How can I improve?

_____

_____

_____

6. Do I make space for couples to unpack their full stories without shame or secrecy? How can I improve?

_____

_____

_____

Couple's Discussion Questions

Discuss the following with your spouse:

1. What parts of our journey could offer the most hope and practical guidance to other couples?
2. How vulnerable are we willing to be in sharing our full story, including our failures and flaws?
3. How can we create space to regularly support other couples without neglecting our own marriage?
4. What mistakes did we make early on that we can help other couples avoid?
5. What key resources or people were instrumental in our healing that we can connect other couples to?
6. What ongoing temptations or vulnerabilities should we monitor in our own relationship so we can assist others with relapse prevention?
7. If we ever feel insufficient to give hope to others, where can we turn for inspiration and renewed vision?
8. How can we fan the flames of our passion to walk with others without growing weary?

NOTES

CONCLUSION

Keep Moving Ahead

I know it hasn't been an easy road walking through the mess addiction created in your life and marriage. But the fact that you're still here seeking hope means you have fight left in you. When we started out together, I assured you that healing is possible even after devastating loss and failure. I've tried to break down some practical tools to equip you for the long journey toward freedom and restoration in your marriage.

My goal has been to tell you that no matter how hopeless your situation feels today, your story isn't over yet. As long as you get up each morning willing to try again, a better chapter lies ahead. With hard work and a circle of support around you, your marriage can be stronger for having navigated these difficult days together.

The tendency once we start seeing progress is to rush impatiently toward some finish line called "normal." But healthy relationships require ongoing effort and growth. Healing is lifelong. Along the way, you'll probably uncover more baggage from your childhood or other issues needing to be unpacked. That's okay! Progress over perfection.

If life were a video game, you'd think there was a final level you could beat that meant you "won" once and for all. But that's not how it goes. Healing from addiction and brokenness in your marriage levels you up over and over, unlocking new growth, ways to cope, and communication skills as you advance. Even years into the future, you'll likely still be discovering areas needing improvement. Now, you have some resources to lean on when those challenges arise.

So, consider this the end of level one, with many more exciting levels ahead. You built the foundation to handle difficulty through accountability, self-care, professional support, communication, and conflict management tools. You defined core values to steer your family and identified harmful generational cycles you are breaking. You discovered the incredible power of being radically honest about your flaws and falling forward.

All those principles set the stage for level two: going even deeper in intimacy and purpose together. Get adventurous! Shake off any lingering shame and protect the progress you have made. Become students of each other. As you feel called and ready, think about how your story could one day inspire other couples still trapped in hopelessness.

Of course, there's no actual "game" manual or guidebook for what comes next. But you have everything you need to keep moving forward: hope, perseverance, accountability, faith, and each other.

Wherever you go from here, make the decision today that you'll do it together. I believe your best days are ahead. But you'll have to keep choosing each other every day. Forgive quickly and give grace freely when tensions inevitably arise. Enjoy the thrill of tackling fresh challenges side by side.

There will be twists and turns in the road, but I believe you will meet them with courage and creativity. Remind each other often that love requires work. Reject complacency in your marriage.

No matter where you're at in your journey today, remember there is hope, and there are resources available. You and your relationship are worth fighting for, so don't give up. Surround yourselves with communities of support. You weren't created to walk this road alone. Together with God, you will get through this. Where human support falls short, His love will carry you. I believe in you!

Personal Reflection

Answer the following questions:

1. What have been the biggest personal lessons I've learned through this book study?

2. What communication or conflict resolution tools do I need the most work on?

3. What feelings arise as I imagine living fully free from addiction's burden?

_____

_____

_____

4. Am I (the addicted spouse) truly serious about doing whatever it takes to walk in freedom?

_____

_____

_____

5. How can I (the supporting spouse) pour hope and empathy into my partner when I feel exhausted?

_____

_____

_____

Couple's Discussion Questions

Discuss the following with your spouse:

1. As we conclude this study, what would each of us say are our biggest takeaways?
2. How have we grown spiritually and relationally over the course of this program?
3. Which communication tools or conflict management tactics still challenge us? How can we strengthen these skills?
4. How often do we celebrate wins versus just focusing on problems? Should we commemorate progress more intentionally?
5. Realistically, what pillars of a recovery lifestyle feel solid versus unstable for us right now?
6. As we look ahead, what brings us the most hope or excitement about addiction no longer controlling our story?
7. If doubts or fears about the future come up, how can we support each other through these emotions with empathy?

8. Do we need to expand our circle of support to receive more encouragement, honest feedback, and wisdom for the path ahead?

9. As we enter this new season focused on intimacy and purpose, what goals or dreams could we explore individually and together? How do we envision actively empowering each other?

ADDITIONAL RESOURCES

The following is a list of suggested resources for ongoing education and support. This list is not inclusive and is not an endorsement of any organization listed. It is provided as a resource. Please use appropriate judgment and caution before seeking help from or joining any organization.

Professional Counseling

American Association of Christian Counselors: www.aacc.net
Christian Association for Psychological Studies: www.caps.net

Recovery and Support Organizations

180 Ministries (Pornography Addiction): www.180recover.com
Adult Children of Alcoholics & Dysfunctional Families: www.adultchildren.org
Alcoholics Anonymous: www.aa.org
Al-Anon & Alateen: www.al-anon.org
American Addiction Centers: www.recovery.org
Anorexics and Bulimics Anonymous: www.aba12steps.org
Be Broken (Sexual Betrayal Recovery): www.bebroken.org
Beyond Ministries (Men's Sexual Addiction): www.beyondthebattle.net
Celebrate Recovery: www.celebraterecovery.com
Co-Dependents Anonymous: www.coda.org
Crystal Meth Anonymous: www.crystalmeth.org
Cocaine Anonymous: www.ca.org
Domestic Shelters: www.domesticshelters.org
Eating Disorders Anonymous: www.eatingdisordersanonymous.org
Emotions Anonymous: www.emotionsanonymous.org
Gamblers Anonymous: www.gamblersanonymous.org
Heroin Anonymous: www.heroinanonymous.org

Marijuana Anonymous: www.marijuana-anonymous.org
Narcotics Anonymous: www.na.org
National Association for Christian Recovery: www.nacr.org
National Domestic Violence Hotline: www.thehotline.org
On-Line Gamers Anonymous: www.olganon.org/home
Overeaters Anonymous: www.oa.org
Pills Anonymous: www.pillsanonymous.org
Pure Desire Ministries (Sexual Betrayal Recovery): www.puredesire.org
Pure Life Ministries (Sexual Addiction): www.purelifeministries.org
Sex and Love Addicts Anonymous: www.slaavirtual.org
Sexaholics Anonymous: www.sa.org
SMART Recovery: www.smartrecovery.org
XXXchurch (Live Free Ministries): www.xxxchurch.com

Recommended Resources from XO Marriage

From Jimmy Evans

Marriage on the Rock 25th Anniversary Edition
The Four Laws of Love
I Will: 365 Daily Promises for Your Marriage
Lifelong Love Affair
Fighting for the Soul of Your Child
Our Secret Paradise
7 Secrets of Successful Families
Blending Families
Blending Families Workbook
Strengths Based Marriage
The Keys to Sexual Fulfillment in Marriage
Vision Retreat Guidebook

From Karen Evans

From Pain to Paradise

From Jimmy & Karen Evans

I Will: 365 Daily Promises for Your Marriage
Fighting for the Soul of Your Child
Vision Retreat Guidebook

From Dave & Ashley Willis

The Naked Marriage
The Counterfeit Climax
Married Into the Family

XO Now

www.xomarriage.com/xo-now/

XO Marriage Conferences

www.xomarriage.com/conferences

GUIDELINES FOR GROUP LEADERS

If you will be using the materials in this book in a small group or a support group for couples, I have included some general guidelines to help you facilitate the process.

State the Purpose

At the beginning of each session, clearly state the purpose of the group: **to support couples dealing with addiction and to rebuild intimacy through shared understanding and accountability.**

Group Format

- I recommend keeping the group relatively small (eight couples maximum) to allow enough time for each couple to share updates and get personalized feedback.
- Meet consistently every week or every other week so members can count on a structured time and space.
- Begin and end each meeting with prayer to invite God's wisdom and healing into every conversation.

Sharing Guidelines

- Have each couple share openly about their journey. However, caution them about protecting privacy in their own marriages around sensitive details.
- Remind members to focus comments on taking ownership of their own choices and behaviors without blaming their spouses.
- Guide couples to identify and celebrate wins since the last meeting, such as days of sobriety, honesty without hiding, quality time together, or any other significant experience that has strengthened their marriage.

- Ask thoughtful questions to prompt the next milestone goals. Explore how group members can support those goals.
- Lovingly challenge any tendencies toward half-measures, spiritual apathy, isolation, self-pity, or anything else that will take away from restoring relationships to health.

Group Feedback

- Stress confidentiality within the group.
- When couples or individuals share their experiences, respond with empathy, compassion, and encouragement.
- Offer practical advice sparingly. Avoid rigid formulas.
- Consistently remind the group members that the desire of God's heart is to redeem and transform lives and marriages.
- Suggest counseling resources, recovery programs, or other supports tailored to each couple's needs.
- You may wish to exchange contact information in the group but only with those couples who consent.

NOTES

Introduction

1. AnnaMarie Houlis, "How Substance Abuse Affects Marriage and Divorce," *Addiction Group,* January 12, 2024, https://www.addictiongroup.org/addiction/divorce/#:~:text=Substance%20abuse%20and%20addiction%20are%20linked%20to%20higher,divorce%20rate%20for%20subsequent%20marriages%20is%20even%20higher.

1. Help! My Spouse Is an Addict!

1. TRESCA, "What's the Difference between Process Addiction and Substance Abuse?," *Teen Rehab,* April 16, 2018, https://www.teenrehab.org/resources/about-addiction/process-addiction-info/.

4. The Right Game on the Right Playground

1. Jim Rohm as quoted in Jack Canfield, et al., *The Success* (New York: HarperCollins Publishers, 2005), 189.
2. Miguel de Cervantes Saavedra, *The Life and Exploits of the Ingenious Gentleman Don Quixote de la Mancha,* Translated by Charles Jarvis, Volume 2, Second Edition, (London: J and R. Tonson and S. Draper, 1749), 134–135.

5. You Can Be the "One"

1. Alyssa Hill, "Sobriety, Relapse, and Addiction Recovery Statistics in 2023," *Addiction Group,* November 27, 2023, https://www.addictiongroup.org/resources/sobriety-statistics/.

7. I'm Sorry

1. Gary D. Chapman and Jennifer Thomas, *The 5 Apology Languages: The Secret to Healthy Relationships* (Chicago, IL: Northfield Publishing, 2022).

8. Lightening the Load

1. Mayo Clinic, "Stress Relief from Laughter? It's No Joke," Mayo Clinic, September 22, 2023, https://www.mayoclinic.org/healthy-lifestyle/stress-management/in-depth/stress-relief/art-20044456.
2. Laura E. Kurtz and Sara B. Algoe, "Putting Laughter in Context: Shared Laughter as Behavioral Indicator of Relationship Well-being," *Personal Relationships* 22, no. 4 (2015): 573–90, https://doi.org/10.1111/pere.12095.

11. Faith

1. Alcoholics Anonymous, "The Twelve Steps," *Alcoholics Anonymous,* https://www.aa.org/the-twelve-steps#:~:text=The%20Twelve%20Steps%201%201.%20We%20admitted%20we,and%20fearless%20moral%20inventory%20of%20ourselves.%20More%20items.

2. Brian J. Grim and Melissa E. Grim, "Belief, Behavior, and Belonging: How Faith Is Indispensable in Preventing and Recovering from Substance Abuse," *Journal of Religion and Health* 58, no. 5 (2019): 1713–50, https://doi.org/10.1007/s10943-019-00876-w.

Printed in the USA
CPSIA information can be obtained
at www.ICGtesting.com
JSHW052042100924
69483JS00002B/10